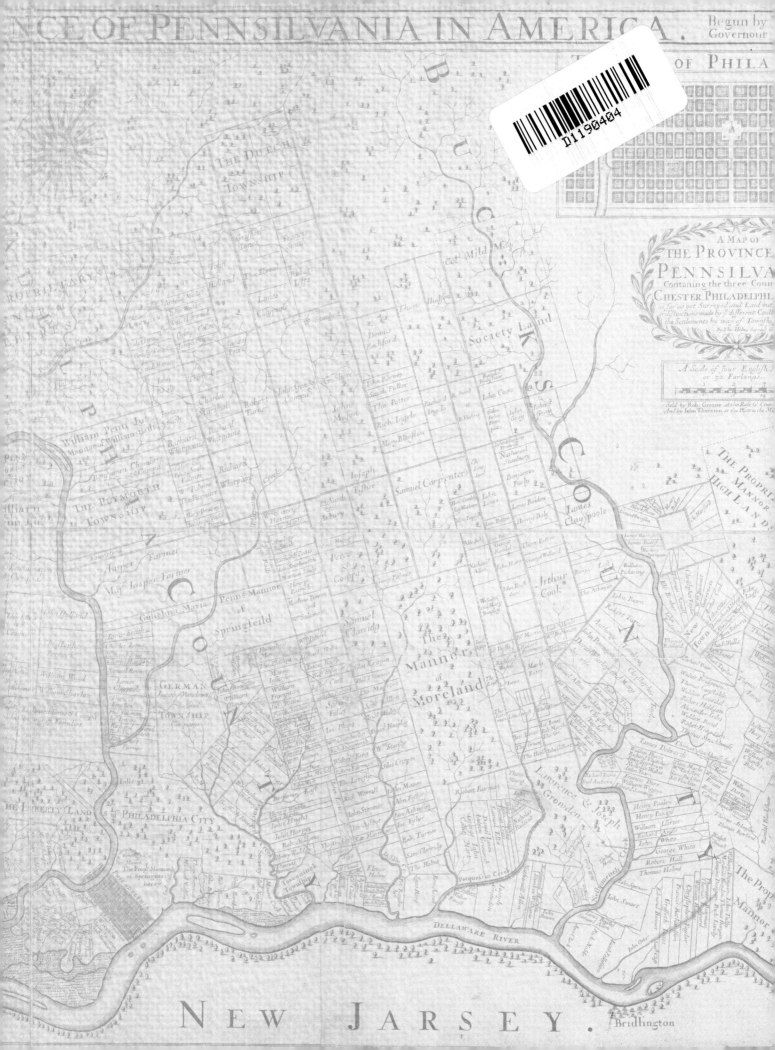

NCE OF PENNSILVANIA IN AMERICA.

Begun by
Governour

OF PHILA

A MAP OF
THE PROVINCE
PENNSILVA
Containing the three Coun
CHESTER PHILADELPHI
as far as yet Surveyed and Land out
distinctions made by 9 different Coul
the Settlements by way of Townshi
By Tho. Holme Su

A Scale of four English
or 32 Furlongs.

Sold by Rob. Greene at the Rose & Crow
And by John Thornton at the Platt in the M

THE PROPRI
MANNOR
HIGH LAND

NEW JARSEY.

Bridlington

DELLAWARE RIVER.

Historic Architecture of Pennsylvania

Written and Photographed by
Scott D. Butcher

Schiffer
Publishing Ltd

4880 Lower Valley Road • Atglen, PA 19310

Adams ~ Cumberland ~ Dauphin ~ Lancaster ~ Lebanon ~ and York Counties

Published by Schiffer Publishing, Ltd.
4880 Lower Valley Road
Atglen, PA 19310
Phone: (610) 593-1777; Fax: (610) 593-2002
E-mail: Info@schifferbooks.com

For the largest selection of fine reference books on this and related
subjects, please visit our website at
www.schifferbooks.com.
You may also write for a free catalog.

This book may be purchased from the publisher.
Please try your bookstore first.

We are always looking for people to write books on new and related
subjects. If you have an idea for a book, please contact us at
proposals@schifferbooks.com.

Schiffer Books are available at special discounts for bulk purchases for
sales promotions or premiums. Special editions, including personalized
covers, corporate imprints, and excerpts can be created in large
quantities for special needs. For more information contact the publisher.

In Europe, Schiffer books are distributed by
Bushwood Books
6 Marksbury Ave.
Kew Gardens
Surrey TW9 4JF England
Phone: 44 (0) 20 8392 8585; Fax: 44 (0) 20 8392 9876
E-mail: info@bushwoodbooks.co.uk
Website: www.bushwoodbooks.co.uk

Copyright © 2012 by Scott D. Butcher
Library of Congress Control Number: 2012947801

Designed by RoS
Type set in Lucida Calligraphy/Book Antiqua
ISBN: 978-0-7643-4275-2
Printed in China

Dedication

For some great friends:

*The Coombes Family
(Lorraine, Jim, Ciara, Grant)
and
The Smith Family
(Loni, Brad, Alex, Nicholas, Oliver)*

Acknowledgments

This book has been a decade in the making, ever since I created a virtual tour of downtown York, Pennsylvania. During the years that followed, I was regularly in touch with the staff of Historic York, Inc., York County's only county-wide non-profit architectural preservation organization. I eventually was elected to the board of directors, serving for four years as secretary and another two as president. In these roles, I had the pleasure of personally working with a number of knowledgeable preservation professionals who all contributed to this book.

Mindy Crawford, who is today the executive director of Preservation Pennsylvania, has always been supportive. Whenever I've called upon her knowledge, she's been happy to share—or at least set me straight! She also happens to be extremely knowledgeable about the Lincoln Highway and architecture of the "recent past," so when I had trouble trying to figure out the maze of "modern" architecture for this book, she happily directed me toward the right path.

Karen Arnold, administrator of the Keystone Historic Preservation Grant Program for the Pennsylvania Historic and Museum Commission, has been another excellent resource. She always responds to my pestering questions and shares ideas with me; over the years, she has not only elevated my knowledge, but also guided me in my search for buildings of various styles.

Barb Raid, an outstanding architectural historian, is a repository of knowledge when it comes to local architecture. Whenever I've asked her a question about a building, an architect, or a style, she has always responded by providing far more information than I anticipated. In fact, while writing this book, I referenced faxes that she sent me many years ago!

Alycia Reiten, the current executive director of Historic York, helped with information for this book by giving her knowledge of architecture, particularly in Cumberland County. Even while I was busy researching, writing, and photographing, Alycia was schooling me about the process of inventorying historic buildings.

Additionally, there are a number of architects whose knowledge has directly impacted this book. Our conversations may have been related to another project or book I happened to be working on at the time, but the lessons they taught were still with me when I began writing *Historic Architecture of Pennsylvania*. These architects include Richard Ward, Tillman Johnson, David McIlnay, Frank Dittenhafer, Hunter Johnson, Steve Funk, John Yoder, Rich Gribble, Dale Yoder, the late John Gilbert, and I'm sure others that I've forgotten.

Without the friendship and knowledge of these people, this would be a far different book. I am grateful to each and every one.

Contents

Introduction

South Central Pennsylvania—the counties of Adams, Cumberland, Dauphin, Lancaster, Lebanon, and York—is an area defined by two major geographic features: a river and hills. The mighty Susquehanna River snakes its way between the area's lazy rolling hills that never grew their way to mountain status. This picturesque countryside provided an attractive backdrop for settlement in the eighteenth century, particularly for immigrants from Germany, who found the topography similar to their homeland.

Lancaster was the first of the local counties, created in 1729 from Chester County. The first European settlement occurred as early as 1710, but English Captain John Smith is known to have visited with the Susquehannock Native American tribe in 1608 while exploring the Chesapeake Bay. Most of South Central Pennsylvania was originally part of Lancaster County, and, one-by-one, the distinctive counties of today were created, beginning in 1749 when York County was established and ending with the creation of Lebanon County in 1813. Together, the six counties cover 3,855 square miles and host a population of almost 1,700,000 residents—roughly the area and population of the Indianapolis-Carmel metropolitan area.

While the U.S. Census Bureau divides South Central Pennsylvania into several separate metropolitan statistical areas, the region often acts as one, commonly referred to as Central Pennsylvania or, more appropriately, South Central Pennsylvania. It is a single media market—HLLY for Harrisburg-

Lancaster-Lebanon-York. The region is not defined by a major city, but rather by several smaller cities that serve as the seat of their respective county: Carlisle, Gettysburg, Harrisburg, Lancaster, Lebanon, and York. A number of other distinctive towns are located in the region, including Hanover, Hershey, Strasburg, and Lititz, to name a few. Harrisburg serves a dual role as both seat of Dauphin County and capital of the Commonwealth of Pennsylvania.

By the time of the American Revolution, Lancaster and York were already established. The British Army defeated General George Washington's Continental Army near Philadelphia in September 1777, forcing the Second Continental Congress to flee Philadelphia for Lancaster, where they spent one day, and then to York, from where they governed the fledgling nation for nine months. During the Civil War, few cities in the North experienced the war firsthand. The exceptions were the towns of South Central Pennsylvania, which first saw a Confederate invasion and occupation in late June 1863, and then witnessed battles in Wrightsville and Hanover, a shelling of Carlisle, and the largest battle ever fought in North America—the Battle of Gettysburg.

The communities of South Central Pennsylvania have played home to craftsmen and builders, artists and inventors, and brilliant industrialists who developed products used throughout the world. In the eighteenth century, the Pennsylvania Rifle and Conestoga Wagon were pioneered in the area. Lancaster County's Robert Fulton invented the first functional steamboat, while York's Phineas Davis developed the first practical coal-burning railroad locomotive. The Pennsylvania Canal along the Susquehanna River, and later railroads like the Pennsylvania Railroad, Philadelphia & Columbia, and Northern Central, allowed the communities of South Central Pennsylvania to become industrial leaders, adding to the region's already strong agrarian roots. Internationally recognized products like Hershey Chocolate, Harley-Davidson Motorcycles, Armstrong Flooring, York Air Conditions, and even Starbucks Coffee are produced in South Central Pennsylvania, demonstrating that the work ethic that was born on the fertile farmland and honed during the Industrial Revolution holds true today.

As the region was developing and growing, education and health care became key community needs, and today, many of the region's largest employers are colleges and healthcare systems. Major public institutions like Penn State, Millersville University, and Shippensburg University are located in the area, as are many well-respected private colleges like Gettysburg College, Franklin & Marshall College, York College of Pennsylvania, and Lebanon Valley College. The Penn State Milton S. Hershey Medical Center is an internationally renowned teaching hospital while the Penn State Hershey Children's Hospital is recognized as one of the best in the United States. Lancaster General Health and York's WellSpan Health have both obtained national recognition for their programs as well as a ranking in *Modern Healthcare's* Top 100 Integrated Health Networks in the United States.

This diverse background provides the framework for the architecture of South Central Pennsylvania. Early settlement by German and, to a lesser extent, British immigrants led to buildings that reflected the architecture of their homelands. Because many of these early buildings were constructed of wood, they no longer stand. Yet there are still many intriguing examples of mid-eighteenth century architecture in the region, including the German-influenced Hans Herr House south of Lancaster and Golden Plough Tavern in downtown York as well as the English-influenced Donegal Presbyterian Church in Mt. Joy and Wright's Ferry Mansion in Columbia.

As more settlers found their way to the area, the architecture became more elaborate. Trinity Lutheran in Lancaster, built in the 1760s, has a steeple that reaches so high that it was, for a period, the tallest building west of Philadelphia. Georgian Style architecture can be found in most communities, but the Federal Style buildings of the late eighteenth century are more prominent and of a higher level of stylistic detail than their simpler predecessors. Old West, on the campus of Dickinson College, is a National Historic Landmark designed by Benjamin Henry Latrobe, best known as architect of the United States Capitol. Wheatland, the home of President James Buchanan, and Schmucker Hall, on the campus of the Lutheran Theological Seminary in Gettysburg, are notable Federal Style buildings with important historical connections.

As the young country matured and prospered, the South Central Pennsylvania region followed. National pride, coupled with community and individual wealth, led to a return to the ideals of ancient Greece, inspiring the Greek Revival style of architecture. Local courthouses were built in the style to showcase community pride, while banks and wealthy businessman constructed large buildings and homes with monumental columns to portray stability and success.

Another architectural movement from Europe was the Gothic Revival, which began in the 1830s and, in one form or another, has continued to this day. Gothic churches with pointed arches are commonplace, but in the nineteenth century a more subtle form of Gothic architecture found its way to domestic buildings. Known as Carpenter Gothic, these wooden homes employed decorated woodwork that would remain in fashion throughout the century. Local churches in this style include St. Stephens Episcopal Cathedral in Harrisburg and the Episcopal Church of St. John the Baptist in York. Most of the wood Carpenter Gothic homes in South Central Pennsylvania are long gone due to the ravages of time; however, Gettysburg's John Rupp House and the Harrisburg Cemetery gatehouse are notable examples.

Most architectural historians group a number of styles under the heading of Victorian, named for British Queen Victoria, who reigned from 1837 to 1901. While the Victorian Era isn't technically a period of American history, it is commonly used when referring to American architecture, beginning with the Italianate Style. Inspired by the rural homes of Tuscany, Italy, Italianate buildings were popular throughout the United States and noteworthy examples can be found in most local communities. Breeze Hill mansion in Harrisburg is perhaps the best regional example of an Italian Villa while Lancaster's Fulton Opera House is a striking building that has obtained National Historic Landmark status. York's Billmeyer House, an urban adaptation of the Italianate Style, is a benchmark in historic preservation law.

Many of the movements in American architecture were inspired by movements in European architecture. After the Second Empire of Napoleon III took control of France in 1852, a new architectural style was born as Napoleon embarked on an aggressive program to transform Paris. The resulting architectural style, identified by a prominent mansard roof, is called Second Empire. It was popular in South Central Pennsylvania in the 1860s and 1870s, with the construction of a number of high style mansions, including Lancaster's West Lawn, Marietta's Riverview, and Harrisburg's Cameron and McCormick Mansions on Front Street. While the style showcased wealth for the period, today, it is associated with ghosts and hauntings thanks to Hollywood's use of the style for the Bates House in *Psycho* and for the Addams Family home.

Whereas the Second Empire Style was heavy and even gloomy, another Victorian style was characterized by a light, even delicate touch. The Stick Style, which is defined by the presence of light decorative sticks, was used almost exclusively for domestic architecture, though architects employed the style for train stations and coastal life-saving stations. The decorative woodwork that was used with the Carpenter Gothic Style was re-interpreted for the Stick Style before again morphing into the Queen Anne Style. Locally, the Stick Style was not prominent, and several stylistic examples that survive today no longer exhibit their tell-tale sticks as their façades have been updated without the decorative enhancements. Harrisburg's Pancake

Row is a collection of eclectic Victorian row houses with decorative stickwork. York's The Avenues neighborhood has several examples that demonstrate the transition from Stick to Queen Anne.

The Queen Anne Style is in many ways the culmination of Victorian architecture, as architects embraced a variety of stylistic details to create grand, even exuberant buildings with front-facing gables, corner towers or turrets, and myriad colors and textures. While the style is most closely identified with residential architecture, schools, farmers markets, and even commercial space embrace the style. Hermansader's Victorian Mansion in Columbia and Gonder Mansion in Strasburg are two excellent examples of Queen Anne architecture while Lady Linden in York embraces the style with a vibrant palette of color and decorative stickwork, exhibiting the transition from the Stick Style.

Gothic architecture, which had become popular in the first half of the nineteenth century, transformed after 1860, as architects combined the flair of the Victorian Era with the more traditional Gothic forms, creating a style known as High Victorian Gothic. This style embraced color and texture, and the resulting polychromatic buildings often combined stone, brick, wood, tile, and shingles—sometimes on a single building. The region's best examples of High Victorian Gothic architecture are both located in Lebanon City—Salem Evangelical Lutheran Church and St. Luke's Episcopal Church.

The appropriately named Shingle Style bridged the late nineteenth and early twentieth centuries. The defining characteristic is a uniform covering of shingles, frequently above a masonry first level. Buildings in this style, usually houses, embrace earth tones and often borrow forms from Queen Anne and Colonial Revival architecture. While there are a number of excellent Shingle Style houses in the area, the style was not nearly as popular as other contemporaneous styles like Colonial Revival and Tudor Revival.

Christian churches in South Central Pennsylvania, and throughout the United States, often incorporate Gothic or Romanesque architectural precedent. Whereas the defining feature of Gothic architecture is the pointed arch, the defining feature of Romanesque buildings is the rounded arch. Romanesque Revival refers to the first wave of round-arched buildings, beginning around 1840. Regional buildings in the style are built of brick or stone and almost always are churches. A reinterpretation of the style by prominent architect H.H. Richardson incorporated monochromatic rough-cut stone buildings with massive arches. The style was successfully employed elsewhere for churches, schools, and public buildings, but was not enthusiastically embraced by local architects. However, another variant of the style, sometimes referred to as Victorian Romanesque, was popular locally and entailed a freer interpretation with multiple textures and colors. The Lancaster Central Market and York Central Market incorporate this style, as do several buildings on the campus of Gettysburg College, Millersville University's Biemesderfer Executive Center, and the Lark Building at the Lancaster Theological Seminary.

While not widely employed by local architects, the Chateauesque Style was used for several grand homes, including the mansions of successful businessmen like Peter Watt and Milton Martin. The Harrisburg Military Post and Colonial Hotel building in York were designed in the style, which did not find widespread use outside of the northeastern United States. The Biltmore House, the largest residence in the country, is the best-known Chateauesqe building in America.

As architecture moved into the final decades of the Victorian Era — or Gilded Age, as the second-half of the Victorian Era is known in America — and into the twentieth century, architects found inspiration in the buildings of Colonial America as well as the architecture of Ancient Greece and Rome. The Italianate Style, which was popular locally in the mid-nineteenth century, morphed into a variant known as Italian Renaissance or Renaissance Revival, inspired by the Palazzi architecture of northern Italy. The style is broad, and was employed for everything from grand homes to government buildings to community centers to churches. Lancaster City Hall, Hershey Community Center, and the Capitol Theatre in York are excellent examples of the style. The Renaissance Revival King Mansion on North Front Street in Harrisburg is one of the most luxurious homes built in South Central Pennsylvania during the early twentieth century.

Because the area played such an important role in early American history — including nine months as capital of the nation in its youth — Colonial Revival architecture is commonplace. Government buildings, libraries, office buildings, mansions, modest houses, churches, and schools showcase the style. While nationally the stylistic period ended in the 1920s, in South Central Pennsylvania the style never went out of popularity, enjoying a resurgence with the American Bicentennial of 1976. Developer-driven neighborhoods are filled with simple interpretations of the style, more appropriately called Neo-Colonial. The Pennsylvania Governor's Residence is Colonial Revival, as are Harrisburg Public Library, Martin Library, the YWCA of Lancaster, and hundreds of other notable local buildings. Industrialist and philanthropist Milton Hershey even constructed his mansion in the style.

Neoclassical Revival and Beaux-Arts Classicism were popular in the early twentieth century and both embraced the classical architecture of Greece and Rome. Neoclassical Revival was the more conservative approach, and used for public buildings and private homes. These buildings employ a temple form and are monumental in appearance with multi-story columns. The North Office Building in Harrisburg as well as the York and Gettysburg Post Office buildings exemplify the style. Named for the École des Beaux-Arts in Paris, Beaux-Arts Classicism is a free-form interpretation of the classical orders. The elaborate style was used to showcase wealth and civic pride. The region's best examples include the Pennsylvania Capitol Building and adjacent Speaker Matthew J. Ryan Legislative Office Building in Harrisburg as well as the façade of the former Watt & Shand Building in Lancaster and Pennsylvania Monument on the Gettysburg Battlefield.

As cities expanded and outer "rings" of residential development were built, new styles were incorporated into the streetscape. Many neighborhoods were developed within city limits beginning in the 1880s. These "streetcar suburbs" may feature Queen Anne and Stick Style homes adjacent to Colonial Revival and Tudor Revival homes, which were more popular after 1900 and more common in the outer rings, often constructed beyond city limits. Tudor Revival buildings have two personalities. The quintessential Tudor building is one with decorative half-timbering; however, only half of the buildings classified as Tudor Revival actually have half-timbers. There are many variants of the style, including grand Jacobean-inspired mansions and quaint Cottswold cottage-like storybook homes. Uptown Harrisburg, School Lane Hills in Lancaster, and Springdale in York all host a number of excellent examples of Tudor Revival architecture, with and without the decorative half-timbering.

With architecture's return to traditional forms, architects of Gothic buildings moved away from the High Victorian flair and back to more conventional interpretations of the style; however, this approach — known alternatively as Late Gothic Revival or Neo-Gothic — resulted in buildings that were typically larger and more elaborate than their mid-nineteenth century predecessors. The style was common for Christian churches, with a variant that was used primarily for educational buildings and known as Collegiate Gothic. Skyscrapers in metropolitan areas also embraced a version of the style. Locally, religious buildings in the Late Gothic Revival Style include Messiah Lutheran and Memorial Lutheran, both in Harrisburg, Union Lutheran and Heidelberg UCC in York, and St. John Lutheran in Lancaster. Examples of Collegiate Gothic include Old Main on the campus of Franklin & Marshall College and the Humanities Building at Lebanon Valley College.

Though not widespread, Spanish Colonial Revival—or Spanish Eclectic—architecture can be found in early twentieth century neighborhoods alongside their more popular Colonial Revival and Tudor Revival siblings. The style encompasses architecture inspired by the Spanish missions of the southwestern United States as well as the stucco-clad, red tile-roofed buildings of Mexico and the Mediterranean. The largest example in South Central Pennsylvania is the imposing Hotel Hershey, but most instances of the style are domestic architecture built in early twentieth-century neighborhoods. York's Elmwood neighborhood has a number of examples, as does Lancaster's School Lane Hills historic district and Uptown Harrisburg.

Just as the French-inspired Chateauesque Style found only minimal acceptance in the region, French Eclectic did not reach the popularity of other concurrent revival styles. The spread of the style was driven by World War I veterans who experienced the beauty of rural France firsthand, and were inspired to live in homes that embraced their character. Local examples can be found in Harrisburg's Bellevue Park, Lancaster's School Lane Hills, and York's Springdale neighborhoods, though Norman Towers on North Front Street in Harrisburg is probably the most visible example.

The revivals of early American and European styles found widespread acceptance in the early twentieth century—throughout the nation and throughout South Central Pennsylvania. However, there was also a growing movement against these traditional forms, and one of the American styles to grow out of this was the Prairie Style pioneered by Frank Lloyd Wright and named by *Ladies Home Journal*. Wright's original goal was to create a style that reflected the prairie terrain of the Midwestern United States through horizontal forms, earth tones, overhanging eaves, and walls that extend beyond building façades. There are a number of examples of the Prairie Style in the region, including one south of New Cumberland designed by a Wright protégé, but local architects did not eagerly design in the style. However, a low-cost alternative, spread via mail-order catalogs, found an audience with developers looking to construct inexpensive, prefabricated homes. This variant, known as American Foursquare, is omnipresent in South Central Pennsylvania.

Another American style of this period is known as Commercial or Chicago School. While early Commercial Style buildings were constructed in New York and Philadelphia, it was the large department stores and office buildings in Chicago that popularized the style nationally. Local architects incorporated the skeletal appearance of the style and then embellished it with features from Beaux-Arts, Italianate, and other styles. Examples include The Bon-Ton and Bear's Department Stores in York, Hager Building in Lancaster, and Dauphin County Veteran's Memorial Office Building.

Two English architects pioneered the Craftsman Style, which caught on in the United States and spread throughout the nation. In California, where real estate was at a premium and developers were looking to build smaller, low-cost homes, bungalows became trendy. And while these small homes incorporated architectural details from a variety of sources, it was the earthy Craftsman features that became associated with the building type. Craftsman/Bungalows became commonplace in suburbs, small towns, and rural areas. Locally, there are simple bungalows everywhere, and the higher style examples often feature Craftsman details. Indian Steps Museum in Airville is one of the most unique Craftsman homes ever constructed, simply because of the presence of hundreds of Native American artifacts incorporated into the walls.

The trend away from traditional styles reached its zenith with the modern movements of the mid-twentieth century. Both Art Deco and Art Moderne were outgrowths of the International Exposition of Modern Industrial and Decorative Arts, which prohibited "reproductions, imitations, and counterfeits of ancient styles," ensuring that new architectural techniques and styles would be developed. Art Deco is angular in form, with vertical orientation and setbacks common. Art Moderne embraces curved forms, with horizontal emphasis and stainless steel. Harrisburg is home to a number of excellent examples of Art Deco, including the Harrisburg Hotel (a.k.a., Fulton Bank Building), Dauphin County Courthouse, Payne Shoemaker Building, and Pennsylvania Farm Show building. Hershey's Catherine Hall and the Hanover Shoe building in southwestern York County also exemplify the style. Art Moderne buildings are less common, though examples exist in most South Central Pennsylvania communities. Royer's Pharmacy in Ephrata and the Modernaire Motel along the Lincoln Highway in east York are noteworthy examples.

Another modern style, known as the International Style, was embraced by European architects first and then spread throughout the world. The style emphasizes modern construction materials and techniques while avoiding ornamentation. One of the most famous architects of the style, Philadelphia's Louis Kahn, designed the Olivetti-Underwood building in Harrisburg. Other local examples include the Pennsylvania Department of Labor and Industry Building and Ronald Reagan Federal Courthouse, both in Harrisburg.

In the early days of American architecture, professional architects were uncommon and buildings were rarely associated with architects or builders. But as the young nation blossomed and expanded, architecture became a profession and notable public and private buildings were often architect-designed, developing the profession and leading to the rise of the architect—locally, regionally, nationally, and even internationally. However, by the mid-twentieth century, buildings became increasingly associated with architectural firms, and not necessarily with a single architect. Name-brand architects are today referred to as "starchitects" as most architectural professionals are employed by the firms that get credited with the designs. This trend away from the singular architect coincided with a trend away from defined styles. Modern architecture, which spans roughly from 1950 to the present, is difficult to characterize or pigeonhole into a particular style. Some have tried, with terms like New Formalism, New-Expressionism, Brutalism, and Post-Modernism, to name a few. Most architectural historians, however, prefer to use the catch-all term of "Modern" to refer to these diverse stylistic designs. Modern can thus be used to refer to the Gettysburg Cyclorama, designed by famed modernist architect Richard Neutra, as well as the Commonwealth Keystone Building in Harrisburg, completed in 2000.

South Central Pennsylvania is blessed with a diversity of buildings, covering almost every style of American architecture from the early 1700s to present-day. Architects today embrace traditional forms as well as new forms and trends, like the environmentally-friendly "green building" movement that began in the 1990s. A number of significant architectural practices are based in the region, enhancing the local built environment while also designing buildings throughout the country and even the world.

It is difficult to not be intrigued by the variety of architecture in South Central Pennsylvania. Architecture helps to define communities by providing a sense of place and creating a connection with the past. Architecture drives tourism, from historic sites like the Ephrata Cloister and Gettysburg to programmatic/roadside icons like the Haines Shoe House and Dutch Haven windmill. Building reuse helps the environment by recycling large structures and minimizing the need for new construction materials while helping the economy by providing jobs for skilled builders. Architecture helps us define who we are, where we've been, and even where we're going. *Historic Architecture of Pennsylvania* captures who we are as a community and our myriad personalities over the past three centuries.

The National Park Service, keeper of the National Register of Historic Places, recommends four books to aid in the identification of architectural styles. While these style guides—as well as the many others available—do not necessarily agree on all stylistic features, terminology, or period, they provide a wealth of information to the casual enthusiast or professional historian. More than one dozen style guides, in print and online, were used to create a consensus description for the styles featured in this book. The chapters are subdivided by periods defined in the National Park Service's *How to Complete the National Register of Historic Places Registration Form*, and the alternative terms are mostly from that publication as well. The years of a particular style's popularity were established after a thorough analysis of the many architectural style guides listed in the bibliography to this book.

Identifying a building's architectural style is part science, part art. There are primary features to look for, but the year a building was originally constructed also plays a role. Alterations over the years may enhance or totally change the character of a building, and thus a building designed in one style may be renovated into a totally different style. Many buildings contain features from two or more styles, and thus are typically identified by the most prominent features. However, architectural historians don't always agree on the classification of a particular building, proving that it isn't always an easy thing to do. Architects practicing today may not have been schooled in styles of American architecture, which is why trained architectural historians are often more closely associated with building classification. Even a review of accepted style guides reveals that the authors sometimes classify the same building in a different style. Further complicating matters is that some even argue that certain stylistic labels are not accurate—for instance, Art Moderne was originally considered a subset of Art Deco, not a unique style. Likewise, some architectural historians now consider the Federal Style to actually be the final phase of Georgian architecture.

Historic Architecture of Pennsylvania breaks out three dozen styles as well as several building types, with multiple photographic examples of each. It is not intended to be a detailed identification guide, but rather an encyclopedia and visual history of the myriad architecture with which the region is so abundantly blessed.

Colonial

English Colonial

Other Terms: Early Georgian; American Colonial; Post-Medieval English
Years: 1600 – 1750

Wright's Ferry Mansion, Columbia, Lancaster County. Reflecting a traditional English design, this sizable stone building was constructed in 1738 for Susanna Wright.

English Colonial is a broad term used to apply to any relatively simple structure built by English settlers and influenced by the buildings of their homeland. Generally, English Colonial refers to a building constructed prior to 1714 (when King George I ascended the throne in England) as well as one that lacks any fancy Georgian ornamentation. However, a simple English-influenced building constructed during the Georgian period may still be considered English Colonial. Features and building material vary by region. In New England, the "New England Colonial" or "Saltbox" is very box-like and typically features a lean-to on one side. Chimneys are frequently located in the center of a small home. Unpainted clapboard siding or weathered, gray shingle siding is common, as are small windows, heavy doors with vertical boards or timbers, second-story overhangs, and steeply pitched gable roofs for snow. A pendant is frequently the only ornamentation. What we today refer to as the Saltbox and the Cape Cod—both popular in seaside settings—are essentially New England Colonials in design.

The "Southern Colonial" is more likely to be brick and have a "T" or "L" shaped plan. Roofs are steeply pitched and chimneys are located at the ends. Façades are symmetrical and bricks laid in either the English or Flemish Bond. A belt course or water table may also be present.

English Colonial buildings in the Mid-Atlantic region are simple buildings, either three bays wide with an off-center door or symmetrical. The "Pennsylvania Farmhouse" is a vernacular type of building that features two front doors, one that opens to an interior hall and a second that provides entrance into a kitchen. Buildings of this type were constructed in the eighteenth and nineteenth centuries, regardless of period or stylistic trends. A pent roof on the front façade, above the first floor, is a common regional feature.

The oldest building in South Central Pennsylvania dates from c. 1719, so all English-influenced buildings technically fall within the Georgian period. However, the Wright's Ferry Mansion in Columbia, Lancaster County, is a notable example of traditional English construction, while the Donegal Presbyterian Church exhibits a Scots-Irish influence. Dauphin County's Paxton Presbyterian Church was built in 1740 and is another noteworthy example.

Paxton Presbyterian Church, Paxtang, Dauphin County. This limestone building, which dates from 1740, replaced a log church constructed eight years earlier. Paxton Presbyterian was restored in 1931 and is one of the oldest continuously-used Presbyterian Church buildings in Pennsylvania.

Donegal Presbyterian Church, Mount Joy, Lancaster County. With its simple design and gambrel roof, this 1732 building reflects the traditions of its Scotch-Irish builders. The size and layout of the church were based upon a meeting house in Ireland's County Donegal.

German Colonial

Other Terms: Medieval Half-Timber, Pennsylvania German Traditional
Years: 1680 – 1800

Hoke-Codori House, Gettysburg, Adams County. This brownstone German Colonial was built in 1786 by Michael Hoke. Today it is home to the Brafferton Inn Bed & Breakfast.

The German Colonial style is prominent in Pennsylvania and Western Maryland, where German immigrants settled, and South Central Pennsylvania probably has the largest extant collection of German Colonial buildings in the United States. A building in this style is frequently more about function than form, leading to unbalanced façades. Floor plans are rectangular, and thick fieldstone or limestone walls are common. Architectural historians sometimes refer to the characteristic floor plan, three rooms on the first floor, as the Continental Plan or *Flurkuchenhaus*. Most examples are two-and-one-half stories with steep, gabled roofs with shingles and central chimneys; pent roofs are sometimes present to shelter the first floor. Shed dormers are also typical. As the various cultures of the American Colonies started to coexist, German Colonial buildings began to incorporate English features, just as Georgian buildings constructed by German craftsman began to exhibit the influence of the builders.

South Central Pennsylvania's oldest building, the Hans Herr House, south of Lancaster City, is an excellent example of a simple German Colonial building. The Ephrata Cloister, a National Historic Landmark, exhibits Germanic architectural influence. In York County, the 1734 Martin Schultz House and 1761 Johannes Cookes House are notable examples of the style. Gettysburg's Hoke-Codori House, today home to Brafferton Inn, was one of the first buildings in the town, which was still part of York County during the period it was constructed.

Top left:
Hans Herr House, Willow Street, Lancaster County. Constructed in 1719 by Christian Herr, the house is named for his father. The landmark building is the oldest in Lancaster County and an exemplary example of the German Colonial style.

Top right:
Johannes Cookes House, York, York County. The limestone Cookes House was built in 1761 by Johannes Guckes (Cookes) and is the third-oldest building in the City of York. It is believed to have been the residence of patriot Thomas Paine while the Second Continental Congress met in York.

Saron, Ephrata, Lancaster County. The Saron, or Sisters' House, was built in 1743 and is part of the Ephrata Cloister, a National Historic Landmark and self-contained religious community developed in the 1730s and '40s.

Golden Plough Tavern, York, York County. The oldest building in the City of York is the home and tavern built by Michael Eichelberger in 1741. Its *fachwerk*, or half-timbering, is unique in the region. It was most likely built as a one-story log house, and then given a second-story addition a few years later.

Aunique subtype of German Colonial is the Medieval Half-Timber or Germanic Half-Timber, which features half-timber construction reminiscent of the homes found in the German Black Forest. Early settlers of Lancaster and York Counties were peasants, and their building techniques were medieval in nature. Known as *fachwerk*, or half-timbering, this post-and-beam construction approach was popular with the German settlers who preferred the simple construction techniques of their homeland. First floors are typically constructed of log or masonry, while second floors feature exposed half timbers with brick or mud chinking. Façades are unbalanced, shingled roofs are steeply pitched, and chimneys are centralized.

Because immigrants from the Palatine region of Germany settled much of the area, half-timbered buildings were prominent into the early 1800s. One of York County's best known buildings, the 1741 Golden Plough Tavern on West Market Street in York, is of the Medieval Half-Timber style, and is certainly one of the best examples of this construction technique in North America. The Klingel House in Strasburg, Lancaster County, is another yet simpler example. Nineteenth century York folk artist Lewis Miller depicted half-timber buildings in many of his drawings, verifying the prominence of this type of construction. However, most buildings have either been lost to the elements and development or covered with siding or even masonry. In Lancaster City, there is an exposed gable on a Howard Street home that exhibits the half-timber construction; however, the entire first floor has been covered by brick.

Friderich Klingel House, Strasburg, Lancaster County. Strasburg's Klingel house is another example of half-timber construction. During a 1986 renovation, the half-timbering was uncovered and the owners found the name Friderich Klingel and the date 1757 carved in a lintel over the door.

An early type of building found in South Central Pennsylvania is the Meeting House (sometimes spelled Meetinghouse), which is descriptive of the building's function, not an architectural style. Many Meeting Houses were built by Friends – or Quakers – and typically reflect an English influence, though the buildings are plain and unadorned. When brick is used, a Flemish bond is common. A simple square floor plan dictated the interior space. Quaker Meeting Houses are not considered sacred houses of worship. In York County, the two most prominent surviving examples are the York Meeting House on East Philadelphia Street in York City and the Warrington Meeting House in Wellsville, though the Redland Friends Meeting House in Newberry Township also survives.

While there is an association between Quakers (Friends) and this type of building, Meeting Houses were also constructed by members of other faiths. Lancaster County has several examples, including the Germanic Saal, which is part of the Ephrata Cloister, a mystical religious community, as well as the Union Meeting House in Marietta, built by Presbyterians. The 1719 Hans Herr House also served as a Meeting House, and is believed to be the oldest surviving Mennonite Meeting House in the United States.

Union Meeting House, Marietta, Lancaster County. This Presbyterian meeting house was constructed between 1816 and 1818 for congregations looking to establish a place of worship.

Saal, Ephrata, Lancaster County. The Saal meeting house at Ephrata Cloister was built in 1741 using the Fachwerk form of construction.

Warrington Meeting House, Wellsville, York County. Built in 1769 and enlarged in 1782, this Quaker Meeting House differs from the one in York because it was built from local fieldstone, not of imported brick.

York Friends Meeting House, York, York County. The original portion of the York Meeting House was constructed in 1766 by the Religious Society of Friends. Bricks were imported from England and laid in Flemish bond. A western addition was built seventeen years later to provide space for women to meet.

The log house is not an architectural style but rather a type of building. As early as the 1720s, German settlers were constructing log homes in South Central Pennsylvania. A log house is built of square timbers hewn from round logs (unlike log *cabins*, which feature round logs). Typical vernacular buildings are of one-and-a-half or two stories and have a gable roof, side doorway, and an end chimney.

One of the best surviving log houses in Lancaster County is the John Phillips House in Lititz, which was part of the Moravian settlement. York County's two-story Barnett Bobb Log House on North Pershing Avenue dates from 1811 and showcases wealth for the period while the tiny Kleiser log house in northern York County is a typical rural example of log construction.

Above Left:
John Phillips House, Lititz, Lancaster County. This two-story log house in Lititz was built by John Phillips in 1796.

Above:
Kleiser Log House, York County. This one-room log house is believed to date from the 1760s and is typical of the tiny log homes built by settlers. The pent roof is original.

Left:
Barnett Bobb Log, York, York County. Remarkable for its size and condition, the Bobb Log House dates from 1811 and spent most of its life several blocks south of its current location, where it is part of the York County Heritage Trust's Colonial Complex.

East Market Street, Marietta Lancaster County. Another example of a two-story log house.

Georgian

Other Terms: Early Georgian; Late Georgian
Years: 1714 – 1780

Named for English Kings George I through IV (1714-1830), the Georgian Style was popular until the American Revolution, at which time architects and builders desired to distance themselves and their designs from the English influence. Georgian architecture is actually based upon English Stuart architecture, in turn based upon the Palladian movement of the Italian Renaissance. The style is sometimes divided into early, middle, and late, or even early and late with 1750 being the dividing year. The Georgian Style in America can be traced to Sir Christopher Wren and James Gibbs, both British architects. The first Georgian building in the American Colonies was completed in 1700 on the campus of the College of William and Mary in Williamsburg, Virginia. The building, today known as the Wren Building, is named for its architect.

Order and balance define the Georgian building, which contains such features as a belt course, water table, lintels with keystones, and quoins. A typical Georgian building is of two stories and three, five, or seven bays wide. The bays are typically in odd numbers to allow for a central doorway to maintain rigid symmetry. However, the "2/3 Georgian" is a subtype common in cramped urban centers. These examples lack symmetry as the doorway is typically not centrally located.

Doorways frequently feature a pediment, entablature, and paneled door. Gable or gambrel roofs are common, and in Pennsylvania, a pent roof is also somewhat common. Early examples feature a steeper pitch while latter examples have flatter roof pitches. Dormers are typical and cornices feature decorative molding. High-style examples also feature rooftop balustrades.

Façades are symmetrical and constructed of fieldstone, clapboard, or brick laid in the Flemish bond. Shutters are frequently absent. End chimneys are common, and differ from the central chimneys favored by the German settlers.

Windows are frequently double-hung – another differentiating feature from German Colonial buildings, which typically used casement windows. As building technology improved, the size of windows increased. Compared with English Colonial buildings, Georgian successors exhibit larger windows. Larger Georgian buildings also frequently feature Palladian windows, a direct influence of the earlier Italian buildings designed by Andrea Palladio, who British and then American architects emulated.

Many Georgian buildings are slightly elevated off the ground, either via a basement level or a platform; this allows use of a water table to help direct water away from the foundation.

The interiors of Georgian buildings are frequently rectangular, two rooms deep with a central hall.

This style is primarily found along the Eastern Seaboard of the United States.

There are numerous Georgian buildings in South Central Pennsylvania, though they are usually smaller and plainer than their counterparts in large urban areas like Philadelphia and Baltimore. Lancaster City has many notable examples, including the Holy Trinity Church, Jasper Yates House, and Sehner-Ellicott-von Hess House. While these examples are all built of brick, Strasburg's Martin Pfoutz House and York's Horatio Gates House are both stone examples of Georgian architecture. The William Willis House in York and John Harris Mansion in Harrisburg also exemplify the style. Perhaps the most unique Georgian home in the region is the polychromatic Checkerboard House, which was built for Valentine Stover north of Lititz, Lancaster County. Pettit's Ford near Dover is built from local red sandstone.

Evangelical Lutheran Church of the Holy Trinity, Lancaster, Lancaster County. This Lancaster church was built in the 1760s, with the tower being added in 1794. The attractive Georgian building was for a time the tallest building west of Philadelphia.

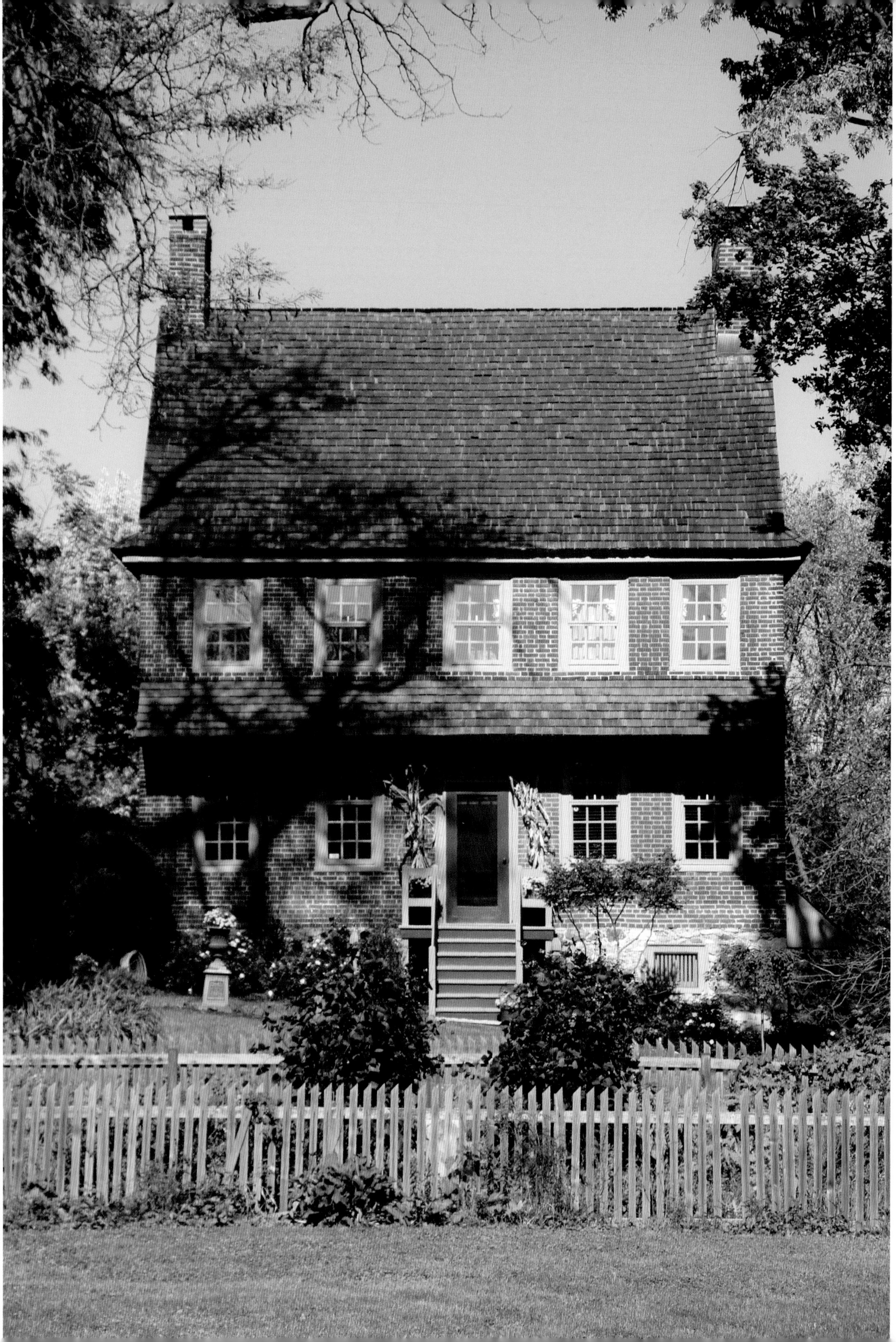

Opposite page:

William Willis House, York, York County. William Willis was a prominent York mason who built the first York County Court House as well as the York Friends Meeting House. His own home was built in 1762, evidenced by the glazed headers with the inscription of "W.W. 1762" in the western gable. Note the pent roof, which is a common feature of Georgian buildings in the mid-Atlantic region. The nearby Horatio Gates House also features a pent roof.

John Harris Mansion, Harrisburg, Dauphin County. The founder of Harrisburg constructed this home between 1764 and 1766. Locally quarried limestone provided the primary building material. President Abraham Lincoln's Secretary of War at the beginning of the Civil War, Simon Cameron, also lived in this house. The North Front Street mansion is a National Historic Landmark.

Checkerboard House, Lititz, Lancaster County. Perhaps the most unique Georgian home in the region is the Checkerboard House, constructed by Valentine Stover in 1754 and located on Route 322 north of Lititz. Incorporating stones of contrasting colors, the home exhibits an unusual polychromatic appearance for the era.

Pettit's Ford, Dover, York County. Located west of Dover, this stately home was built in 1798 and demonstrates how an architectural style, in this case Georgian, can continue to be in vogue locally, long after the stylistic period has ended nationally. It is notable for its use of red sandstone, a common building material in northern York County and southern Cumberland County.

Early Republic

Federal

Other Terms: Adams; Adamesque
Years: 1780 – 1820

Wheatland, Lancaster Township, Lancaster County. The mansion associated with James Buchanan, fifteenth president of the United States of America, was actually constructed in 1828 by William Jenkins, a Lancaster attorney. The Federal mansion is today a National Historic Landmark and open for tours.

The Federal Style began after the American Revolution and continued well into the 1800s. It is characterized by a rejection of the ornamentation and detailing of Georgian architecture, and, more importantly, was meant to be a new Federal Style for the new country. Architects were eager to distance their work from the Georgian Style that was so connected with England; however, the Federal Style actually comes from the British Adams Brothers, for whom the style is sometimes named and whose work was spread throughout the United States via pattern books.

While the Federal Style has many similarities with the Georgian Style, it is lighter and less formal than its predecessor. The first Federal application in America was the dining room at George Washington's Mount Vernon estate. At first glance, Federal Style buildings appear similar to Georgian, which is why some architectural historians refer to Federal as the final phase of Georgian.

Round or oval shapes entered the design vocabulary through such features as rounded walls, semi-elliptical fanlights, Palladian windows, and curved, wrought-iron railings.

Buildings are rectangular or square in shape and often three stories in height, though each successive story is shorter than the one below. Roofs are side gabled or hipped with minor pitches. Balustrades or roof dormers with arched windows are also common. Façades are generally symmetrical and comprise clapboard or feature Flemish bond brickwork. End chimneys are present, and more slender than their Georgian counterparts.

Windows are larger and more frequent than with Georgian buildings, though window panes are smaller than their predecessors.

Common decorative features include stone lintels with keystones, belt courses, swags, flowers, and even urns set atop a roofline.

Doorway features include pilasters, porticos, fanlights, sidelights, and/or transoms.

Great examples of Federal Style architecture can be found throughout South Central Pennsylvania. President James Buchanan's Lancaster home, known as Wheatland, is an excellent example of a large, elaborate Federal home. The tiny Guinston Presbyterian Church, located in southern York County, is built of fieldstone and incorporates Federal features. In downtown Lancaster, the Old City Hall building on Penn Square is a larger example of Federal architecture while the Thaddeus Stevens and Neff-Passmore houses are more typical examples of the style. Schmucker Hall, on the campus of the Lutheran Seminary at Gettysburg, is famed for its role in the early fighting of the Battle of Gettysburg, but is also a notable Federal Style building. Front Street in Harrisburg has several examples, including the Fort Hunter Mansion north of town and the Macklay Mansion, an atypical stone Federal building.

Old City Hall, Lancaster, Lancaster County. The Public Office House was built on Lancaster's Penn Square in 1795-1797 and showcases the Federal Style with Flemish-bond brickwork. The building also housed the state government from 1799 to 1812.

Old West, Carlisle, Cumberland County. Benjamin Henry Latrobe, architect of the United States Capitol and one of the country's first professional architects, designed this three-story limestone building in 1803. Construction commenced the following year, but it was not fully completed for almost two decades. Old West, on the campus of Dickinson College, was named a National Historic Landmark in 1969.

Thaddeus Stevens House, Lancaster, Lancaster County. Thaddeus Stevens, a Radical Republican known as "The Great Commoner," built this house in 1843 and lived here until his death in 1868.

Schmucker Hall, Gettysburg, Adams County. Known as the "Old Dorm," this building, located on the campus of the Lutheran Theological Seminary at Gettysburg, is famous for its role on the first day of the Battle of Gettysburg. However, it is also notable as a large Federal Style building dating from 1832. The original cupola was destroyed by lightning in 1913.

Classical Revival

Other Terms: Jeffersonian Classicism; Roman Revival; Early Classical Revival; Roman Classicism
Years: 1780 – 1850

Leaman Mansion, Paradise, Lancaster County. Located along the Lincoln Highway, near Paradise, the Leaman Mansion is an example of the Classical Revival style. The Palladian Window in the pediment of the 1839 building is a differentiator from Greek Revival buildings, which feature plain pediments.

Classical Revival buildings in the United States were designed or inspired by Thomas Jefferson, who in turn found his inspiration from the work of Italian architect Andrea Palladio and ancient Roman ruins. Jefferson believed the Georgian Style was too English for the new nation. The most famous American building in this style is Monticello, Thomas Jefferson's residence.

The National Trust for Historic Preservation uses the phrase "Early Classical Revival" to characterize Roman-inspired buildings from this period and "Classical Revival" to refer to early twentieth-century buildings that incorporate both Greek and Roman features. Some architectural historians refer to this style as "Neoclassical," while a number of style guides use "Classical Revival" as a catch-all category to include both early Greek and Roman influenced buildings. For this book, the phrase refers to those buildings with a distinctly Roman inspiration, and buildings in South Central Pennsylvania that meet this criteria are exceedingly rare.

Classical Revival buildings are monumental and frequently have a shallow dome. Classical white porticos are common, as is a pediment with half-round window in the tympanum. Columns are either Roman Doric or Tuscan, façades are balanced, and roofs are frequently low and hipped. Roof balustrades are also common. Exterior finish may be brick, stucco, or stone, though the "red brick façade with white portico" is the most common association of the style. Greek Revival was a far more common style across the young nation, and the presence of arched openings and domes help differentiate Classical Revival buildings from their Greek Revival counterparts.

The area's best example of Classical Revival is the Leaman Mansion, which is located along the Lincoln Highway just east of Paradise, Lancaster County. The Palladian window is a giveaway that the style is Roman and not Greek. The 1852 Lancaster County Courthouse has also been noted to be a Roman-based building, as that was the preference of architect Samuel Sloan; however, the prominent Corinthian columns are more Greek because they are fluted; Romans typically used smooth Corinthian columns. In York, Elmwood Mansion features a curved porch lined with Roman Doric columns.

Elmwood Mansion, Spring Garden Township, York County. This plantation home was built in 1835 and relocated approximately two blocks to its current location in 1905. Built by Jacob Brillinger, the mansion was once part of a large complex that included a barn, mill, and creamery.

Lancaster County Courthouse, Lancaster, Lancaster County. This prominent building was built in the 1850s from a design by nationally-noted architect Samuel Sloan, whose practice was based in Philadelphia. The building's massive dome shows a Roman influence.

Greek Revival

Other Terms: Sometimes lumped under the "Classical Revival" category
Years: 1820 – 1860

Donegal Mills Plantation, Mount Joy, Lancaster County. The original portion of this eastern Lancaster County house was built prior to 1790; however, it didn't receive its Greek Revival appearance until a major 1830 addition, which included construction of the monumental Greek Ionic Order portico. Greek Revival is the favored style of the quintessential "southern plantation," and this building would certainly look at home in the deep South.

This style of architecture is an attempt to emulate the Greek "temple" form and is important as much for its political statement as for its architectural features. In the early 1800s, the United States was still a young nation. Many Americans were enamored with the democratic ideals of ancient Greece, so architects looked to early Greek architecture for inspiration. The pioneer of Greek Revival in the United States was architect Benjamin Henry Latrobe, who was born in England and moved to the U.S. His design for the Bank of Philadelphia is the first American building in the Greek Revival style, though his contribution to the local area, Old West at Dickinson College, is Federal in style. Many public buildings in Washington, D.C. were designed in this style, with perhaps the best-known example being the United States Treasury.

For major public buildings, a gabled portico with low-pitched roof is commonly used to emulate the Greek temple form, though flat roofs are also prevalent. The gabled end almost always faces the street, unlike Federal and Georgian buildings, which are commonly side-gabled. Doric, Ionic, or even Corinthian columns or pilasters, along with Greek entablatures and prominent cornices, help to define the style. There is a general "heaviness" in Greek Revival buildings due to the columns, heavy cornices, and substantial window surrounds.

Chimneys, when present, are frequently not visible from the front of a building while roof dormers are rarely present.

Doorways are typically elaborate, with pilasters or engaged columns, rectangular transoms, sidelights, and appropriate design features like Greek frets. Doorways are frequently recessed.

First story windows are taller than second story windows, which are in turn taller than third story windows. Small attic windows are common.

White is the most prominent color, and is found on columns, pilasters, molding, pediments, and even façades. For domestic buildings constructed of wood, façades are typically white. In fact, the stereotypical "southern plantation" is actually a Greek Revival mansion.

While people often think of massive public buildings or mansions in the style, Greek Revival found its way into smaller urban townhouses by combining a Federal style façade with a prominent Greek Revival entrance that embraces the temple form. Greek details may also be present in the window and door surrounds. For these examples, a white entrance contrasts with a red-brick façade. Larger examples are symmetrical with a central entrance while smaller urban examples may be three-bays wide with the entrance to the left or right of center.

Greek Revival was popular in South Central Pennsylvania, evidenced by the number of surviving examples. Many prominent buildings, like the second York and Dauphin County courthouses, have been demolished. The Donegal Mills plantation in western Lancaster County typifies the southern plantation while the Harrisburg YWCA building represents the massiveness of the temple form. Pennsylvania Hall, on the campus of Gettysburg College, and the Cumberland County Courthouse in Carlisle, both pre-date the Civil War and are notable local examples. The Grubb Mansion, better known as home to the Lancaster Museum of Art, and Small Mansion, today called the Lafayette Club in York, are domestic adaptations of the style.

Dauphin Deposit Bank, Harrisburg, Dauphin County. Architect Samuel Holman designed this building for Harrisburg Savings Institution, later renamed Dauphin Deposit Bank. The 1839 building showcases the "temple form" of Greek Revival.

Sylvan Heights Mansion, Harrisburg, Dauphin County. Better known as the Harrisburg YWCA, this Greek Revival mansion was constructed in 1835 by John H. Brant. Nicknamed "The Acropolis of Harrisburg" because of both its architectural style and location on a hill overlooking the city, the building didn't receive its gabled roof until a 1901 renovation project.

Right top:
Pennsylvania Hall, Gettysburg, Adams County. Known in the early days as the College Edifice, this was the first building on the campus of Gettysburg College. The prominent cupola is believed to have been used by Confederate General Robert E. Lee to survey the area during the Battle of Gettysburg.

Right bottom:
Cumberland County Courthouse, Carlisle, Cumberland County. The "old" courthouse was constructed in 1846 and features fluted Corinthian columns built of sandstone. The building was struck by at least one artillery shell during a Confederate barrage on the night of July 1, 1863. A replacement courthouse was constructed nearby in 1962 and the former courthouse now houses county offices.

Gothic Revival

Other Terms: Early Gothic Revival
Years: 1830 – 1870

John Rupp House, Gettysburg, Adams County. Located in Gettysburg, this Gothic Revival home was built in 1868 to replace an earlier Rupp family home that had been heavily damaged during the Battle of Gettysburg. Its three prominent gables all feature decorative bargeboard with the quatrefoil design.

Gothic Revival architecture drew inspiration from the cathedrals and castles of Medieval Western Europe, in contrast to other styles that emulated the older Greek and Roman precedents. Initially, the style was primarily used for masonry churches; however, it was eventually adopted for wood houses (sometimes called Carpenter's Gothic or Gothic Cottages), colleges (Collegiate Gothic), and even an eclectic polychromatic interpretation for public buildings (Victorian or Ruskinian Gothic).

The defining feature of a Gothic Revival building is the pointed arch, which may be lancet (a.k.a., Gothic), Tudor, ogee, or even triangular.

Buildings in this picturesque style have a vertical orientation, and much of the visual emphasis is along the roofline. Roofs are steeply pitched and feature intersecting gables or central gables. Towers with battlements are common, particularly on ecclesiastical buildings. Polygonal chimney pots, pointed dormers, cast iron cresting on roof ridges, and finials define the roofline.

Tall, narrow windows are arched and feature tracery or diamond panes, leaded or stained glass, and hood molds. Bay and oriel windows are common. Columns, if present, may be clustered.

Andrew Jackson Downing's book, *The Architecture of Country Houses* (1850), popularized the use of Gothic Revival for houses. Wood homes in the style are typically asymmetrical and frequently feature earth-toned vertical siding, decorative barge boards at the roof eaves, brackets, railings, and plenty of "gingerbread." Porches may span the full width of a front façade or only a portion of it, and entrances include Gothic features.

In South Central Pennsylvania, Gothic Revival was popular for churches, as was its successor, Late Gothic Revival. York's original Masonic Temple on North Beaver Street in an excellent urban adaptation of the style while the Episcopal Church of St. John the Baptist and St. John's Evangelical Lutheran Church, both in downtown York, are two brick examples. Harrisburg's brick Episcopal Cathedral on Front Street shows Gothic Revival in its simplistic form, a vastly different appearance than exhibited by the Gothic buildings of the Victorian period that followed. The gatehouse at Harrisburg Cemetery, Dwen Cottage in Carlisle, and John Rupp House in Gettysburg are all examples of the Carpenter Gothic interpretation of the style.

Harrisburg Cemetery, Harrisburg, Dauphin County. The caretaker's house of this historic cemetery is a notable example of Carpenter Gothic architecture, complete with bargeboard under the eaves as well as pointed arch and flat arch hood molds. The wood building was constructed in 1845. Note the quatrefoil window in the center gable; the pattern that represents a flower with four lobes was a popular form of Gothic Revival ornamentation.

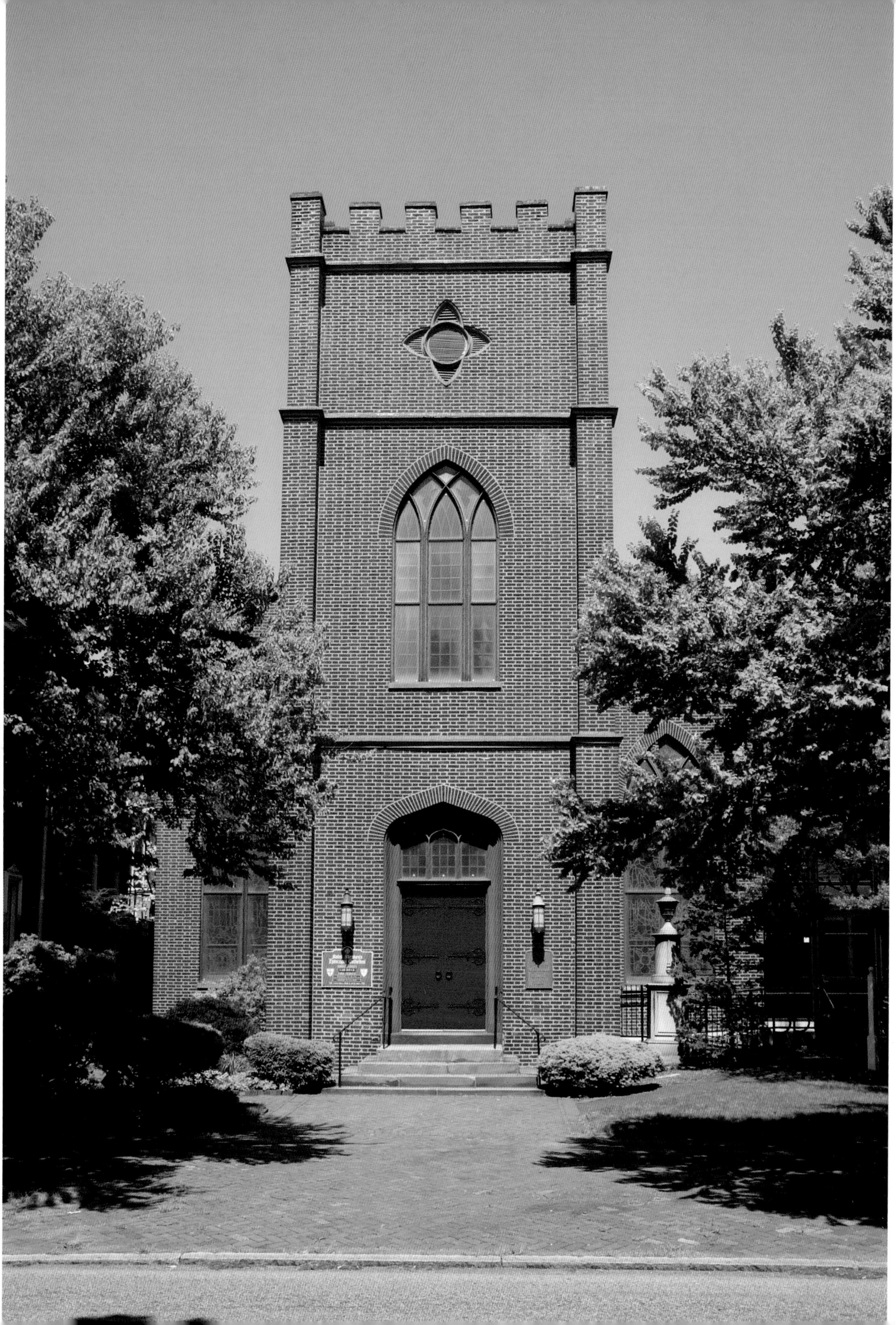

Opposite page:
St. Stephen's Episcopal Cathedral, Harrisburg, Dauphin County. The Episcopal Cathedral Church was constructed on Harrisburg's Front Street in 1827. It showcases the early, more simplistic and reserved phase of Gothic Revival architecture and its appearance is largely unchanged today.

Masonic Hall, York, York County. York's original Masonic Hall was constructed in 1863 by the owner of an adjacent hotel. The building features prominent hood molds exhibiting the lancet arch; interestingly, the building takes a cue from Romanesque Revival buildings, which often featured arched corbel tables under the eaves. The Masonic Hall building employs the technique, but uses the Gothic or lancet arch instead of the round arch found on Romanesque buildings.

Exotic Revival

Other Terms: Exotic Eclectic
Years: 1835 – 1890; 1920 – 1930

Prospect Hill Cemetery, North York, York County. Designers of the Vermont Marble mausoleum at York's Prospect Hill Cemetery drew influence from the architecture of ancient Egypt, incorporating two types of Egyptian columns as well as sphinxes guarding the entrance. The structure was built in 1915 by the American Mausoleum Company from Cleveland, Ohio, with local professional Edward Leber serving as supervising architect.

Beth Israel Synagogue, York, York County. York's first Jewish temple was built in 1907 from a design by Charles Keyworth. The copper onion domes help define the building as Exotic Revival, incorporating an Eastern European architectural feature.

Dauphin County Veteran's Memorial Obelisk, Harrisburg, Dauphin County. Located in Italian Lake Park, this obelisk was built in 1866-1867 as a tribute to Civil War soldiers. The monument stands at 110 feet and incorporates 600 tons of stone quarried on the banks of the Susquehanna River. The obelisk was originally located in a park at North Second and State Streets, and was relocated in 1960.

Exotic Revival is an extremely broad style – an attempt by architects to incorporate design characteristics from throughout the world. In fact, many Exotic Revival buildings combine features from multiple styles. Influences include Egyptian, Moorish, Indian, Turkish, and Byzantine architecture. The Swiss Chalet is sometimes even lumped into this style, though it is decidedly less exotic. Exotic Revival architecture can be found in everything from mausoleums to homes to theaters. In fact, there was a revival of Exotic Revival architecture in the 1920s as movie palaces around the country were constructed in the style. Grauman's Chinese Theater, the Mayan Theater, and the Egyptian Theater are all famous examples located in Los Angeles and Hollywood.

Turkish onion domes and Egyptian columns are popular applications of the style. Jewish synagogues were sometimes constructed in a Moorish style to differentiate them from the Romanesque and Gothic-influenced Christian churches. The Washington Monument, an Egyptian obelisk, is perhaps the most famous Exotic Revival structure in the United States.

In general, local architects shied away from the exotic styles, though there are a handful of Exotic Revival buildings in South Central Pennsylvania. These include the North African-influenced Zembo Shrine in Harrisburg and Egyptian-influenced Prospect Hill Cemetery mausoleum in York, as well as Harrisburg's own obelisk, the Dauphin County Veteran's Memorial Obelisk. Turkish onion domes can be found on several regional buildings, including York's original Temple Beth Israel.

Zembo Temple, Harrisburg, Dauphin County. The unique Zembo Temple was dedicated in 1930 and designed by Charles Howard Lloyd, who used the architecture of northern Africa, particularly Morocco, as his inspiration for the building's appearance.

Italianate

Other Terms: Italian Villa; High Victorian Italianate
Years: 1830 – 1890

Billmeyer House, York, York County. The Charles Billmeyer House is a notable example of the urban townhouse subtype of Italianate. More importantly, the fight to keep the building from being demolished became a national benchmark in preservation law, going all the way to the Pennsylvania Commonwealth Court. First Presbyterian Church of York v. City Council of York was a landmark test of local preservation law and the power of historic architectural review boards.

The Italianate Style is broadly used to encompass the Italian Villa, Italian townhouse, Italian Palazzi (a.k.a., Italian Renaissance Revival), and Commercial Italianate. Nineteenth-century American architects, along with writers, sculptors, and painters, were fascinated with Italy in general and the ancient Roman ruins in particular. The rural homes and farmhouses in Tuscany provided further inspiration. Landscape designer Andrew Jackson Downing, author of popular pattern books, helped popularize the style in his work, *The Architecture of Country Houses*, which included patterns created by Andrew Jackson Davis.

Italianate buildings are generally vertical and asymmetrical in appearance.

Moderate and low-pitched roofs with wide eaves are characteristic, and a defining feature of the style is the presence of ornate decorative brackets under the eaves. These brackets frequently appear in pairs. Roofs are most often hipped or gabled. Chimneys feature ornate caps.

Façades are frequently of brick, often rough cast, and sometimes covered in stucco. The color palate is drawn from earthly hues. Corner quoins add further character to façades.

Windows are tall and narrow, and frequently feature arches and decorative hood molds. As with the brackets, windows are often paired. Oriels are also common.

Entrances are elaborate, and often feature paneled double-doors flanked by classical columns or pilasters.

The Italian Villa, inspired by the country homes of northern Italy, was the first of the subtypes to have an impact in American architecture. Frequently "L" or "T" shaped, the Italian Villa is defined by a tower.

The Villa is typically more elaborate than its urban sibling, and sometimes features arcaded porches.

The townhouse subtype is often square or rectangular and has three or four stories, but no tower is present. Rather, a cupola – or lantern – is common. Italian Palazzi architecture morphed into the Italian Renaissance Revival, covered elsewhere in this book. The Commercial subtype expands upon the townhouse and frequently features cast iron façades and a raised pediment or parapet above the roofline. The Italianate Style was so popular that it was occasionally mixed with other styles, like Gothic Revival. While the term "Brownstone" is used to generically refer to an urban townhouse constructed of brownstone, the characteristic "Brownstone" townhouse is frequently Italianate in style.

Italianate was extremely common in South Central Pennsylvania. Harrisburg's Breeze Hill is an excellent example of an Italian Villa. York's Billmeyer House, an exemplary example of the townhouse subtype, is a national benchmark in historic preservation because it was at the center of a landmark case heard by the Pennsylvania Commonwealth Court after the City of York denied a church's request to demolish the historic building. Lancaster's Fulton Opera House is a National Historic Landmark theater designed in the Italianate Style. The Rex and Laurel Fire House in downtown York is one of the most picturesque and longest-occupied firehouses in the United States and draws influence from Italian Villa and Gothic Revival architecture. Also in York is the former *York Dispatch* Newsroom Building, which features a cast iron façade and exemplifies the Commercial Italianate subtype. The Gettysburg Train Station is perhaps the most visited Italianate building in the region.

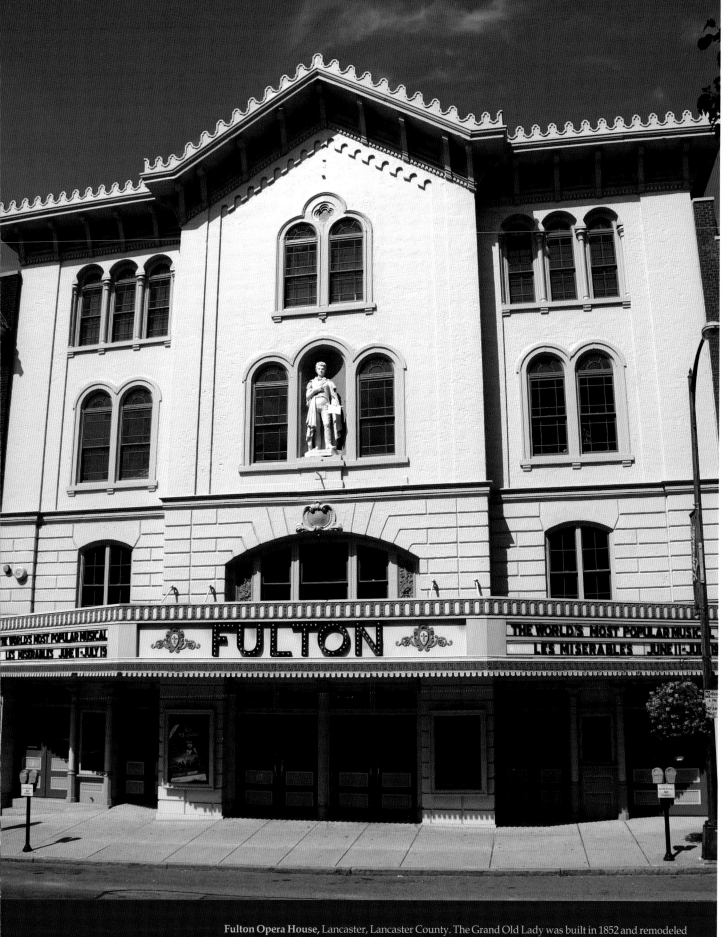

Fulton Opera House, Lancaster, Lancaster County. The Grand Old Lady was built in 1852 and remodeled in 1873, when its name was changed from Fulton Hall to Fulton Opera House. The Italianate building was named a National Historic Landmark in 1969. The original design was completed by Samuel Sloan, who was an author of several popular books and a proponent of the Italianate style. The renovation was designed by Edwin Forrest Durang, a well-known architect of theatrical and ecclesiastical buildings.

Breeze Hill, Harrisburg, Dauphin County. This high-style example of an Italian Villa was built in 1876 as a summer residence for Jacob Haehnlen, who established the Belle Vue Winery. The bracketed tower establishes the home as a Villa. J. Horace McFarland, founder of the American Civic Association and American Rose Society, also lived here.

Rex and Laurel Fire Station, York, York County. The original portion of the picturesque Rex and Laurel Fire Station was constructed in 1878 as the Laurel Engine House. Ten years later, the building was expanded to include space for the Rex Hook & Ladder Company. Designers of the firehouse incorporated Italianate features, added a tower inspired by Italian Villa architecture, and included Gothic windows on the tower's third story and roof openings. This style combination is sometimes referred to as Italianate-Gothic.

Second Empire

Other Terms: Mansard; General Grant Style; Second Empire Baroque
Years: 1855 – 1890

Riverview, Marietta, Lancaster County. One of South Central Pennsylvania's best known examples of Second Empire style architecture is Riverview, the 1860 stone mansion that stands along Route 441 near Marietta.

When the Second Empire of Napoleon III assumed control of France in 1852, Napoleon set out to make Paris an international capital of style. Austrian Baron Georges Eugene Haussman was hired to make this dream a reality; soon, grand boulevards and imposing structures were being built, and the world began to take notice. The 1852-1857 expansion of the Palais du Louvre in Paris is the most famous example of the style in the world, while Philadelphia City Hall is one of the most notable American examples. American architects attending the Paris Exhibitions of 1855 and 1867 were introduced to the Second Empire Style, which they brought back to the United States.

The defining feature of the style is the mansard roof, a two-pitched roof with flat upper slope and a steep lower slope, resulting in a usable attic story. Named for François Mansart, a seventeenth-century French architect, the mansard roof allowed Parisian architects a way to add an extra story to a building without violating the strict height laws. The Second Empire Style, which in many ways is the Italianate Style with a mansard roof, is considered a high style of the Victorian Period.

The mansard roof, which could be concave, convex, or even straight, commonly features wide eaves with Italianate-style brackets. Slate is the roofing material of choice and fish scale patterns are frequently employed. Cast iron cresting and decorated dormers further emphasize the roof as a prominent attribute.

While façades can be asymmetrical, more often buildings are balanced and feature a projecting central pavilion. Prominent quoins embellish building corners and a belt course with a contrasting color is often present.

Tall first-story windows may reach to the floor level and upper level windows are typically double hung with large panes of glass and arches, either in the windows themselves or pediments. Triangular window pediments are also common.

Classical molding and columns may also adorn façades, and entryways incorporate heavy double doors with porches or paired columns.

There are many high-style examples of Second Empire Style buildings in South Central Pennsylvania. Harrisburg's Front Street features several notable mansions in the style, including the James Cameron Mansion and James McCormick Mansion. Lancaster City's West Lawn on West Chestnut Street and Sprenger Brewery Building on East King Street typify the style. Marietta's Riverview and Maytown's Grove Mansion also exhibit the picturesque features of this High Victorian Style. In York City, block after block of townhouses feature mansard roofs and bracketed eaves.

James McCormick Mansion, Harrisburg, Dauphin County. The president of Dauphin Deposit Bank, James McCormick, constructed this stately limestone mansion in 1869 on North Front Street in Harrisburg.

J. Donald Cameron Mansion, Harrisburg, Dauphin County.
This picturesque limestone Second Empire home was built in
1863 and purchased seven years later by J. Donald Cameron,
the U.S. Secretary of War under President Ulysses Grant.

West Lawn, Lancaster, Lancaster County. One of the founders of Millersville Normal School, Barton Bowman Martin, built this striking home on West Chestnut Street in Lancaster in 1874.

Stick/Eastlake

Other Terms: Eastern Stick; High Victorian Eastlake
Years: 1850 – 1890

A MAP OF
PENNSYLVANIA
EXHIBITING
not only THE IMPROVED PARTS of that PROVINCE, but also
ITS EXTENSIVE FRONTIERS:
...down FROM ACTUAL SURVEYS,
...FROM THE LATE MAP of W. Scull Published in 1770;
And Humbly Inscribed
TO THE HONOURABLE
THOMAS PENN AND RICHARD PENN ESQUIRES
AND ABSOLUTE PROPRIETARIES & GOVERNORS OF THE
PROVINCE OF PENNSYLVANIA
and the TERRITORIES thereunto belonging.
English Miles 69¼ to a Degree.

Pancake Row, Harrisburg, Dauphin County. Alfred Pancake constructed this row of picturesque Victorian townhouses in the late 1880s in the Shipoke neighborhood of Harrisburg. Though quite eclectic in appearance, they do exhibit a number of Stick features, including vertical orientation, front-facing gables, and the decorative "sticks" associated with the style.

The Stick Style evolved from Carpenter Gothic and became popular in the mid-nineteenth century. Many architectural historians view it is a transitional style bridging Carpenter Gothic with Queen Anne. It was a uniquely American style, in contrast to the European influenced styles popular at the same time. The distinguishing characteristic of a Stick building is the presence of horizontal, vertical, and diagonal decorative sticks, which are lighter than the half-timbers used in Tudor Revival buildings. These sticks are used to outline the various planes on a building – windows, doors, bays, and corners. Cape May, New Jersey and Newport, Rhode Island, feature some of the country's best examples of Stick architecture.

The typical Stick building, which is almost always a residential building, is asymmetrical and has a vertical orientation. Steep gabled roofs are emphasized through cast iron cresting, polygonal turrets, dormers, and finials. Exposed rafters or decorative brackets under the eaves are also common. Many examples feature intersecting gabled roofs and gabled dormers. Chimneys may be present though not prominent.

With the exception of the decorative stickwork, façades are typically unadorned and feature horizontal wood siding. Large porches and verandas are common, and porch supports may be unadorned or feature scroll sawn elements. Colors are subdued and range from white to earth tones, with the decorative sticks usually painted in a contrasting color. Windows are tall, unadorned, and feature large panes.

Eastlake is a style of *ornamentation*, not an architectural style. Pioneered by Charles Locke Eastlake – an English interior designer well-versed in Gothic Revival architecture and author of the 1868 book that inspired the movement, *Hints on Household Taste* – Eastlake ornamentation is common on Queen Anne and Stick buildings. The National Trust for Historic Preservation combines Stick and Eastlake into a subcategory of Late Victorian architecture. Features include curved brackets and scrolls at corners, latticework along porch eaves, massive porch posts resembling table legs, and rows of spindles on porches or verandas. Ironically, Charles Locke Eastlake was not a fan of the way Eastlake ornamentation was incorporated into American architecture, commenting that it was both extravagant and bizarre.

Because Eastlake ornamentation is primarily constructed of wood, much of this picturesque architectural embellishment has been lost to weather, rotting, and time in general. However, Eastlake examples do exist, including Past Purrfect Bed & Breakfast in Jacobus and several examples in York's The Avenues neighborhood. Many of the best examples of Queen Anne and Stick in South Central Pennsylvania also feature Eastlake detailing, particularly on the front porches.

While there are examples of Stick buildings in South Central Pennsylvania, it was not a favored local style. Several examples can be found in York's historic neighborhood The Avenues, and one of Harrisburg's most photographed blocks is Pancake Row in Shipoke, a collection of colorful, eclectic buildings with decorative sticks.

The Avenues, York, York County. This home, located on Linden Avenue in York's The Avenues neighborhood, has been renovated but still showcases the distinguishing features, including asymmetrical form, vertical orientation, polygonal corner tower, brackets under the eaves, and light stick ornamentation in horizontal and vertical form.

Past Purrfect Bed & Breakfast, Jacobus, York County. The home of Frederick and Henrietta Emenheiser was built in the late nineteenth century, incorporating the picturesque detailing inspired by Charles Eastlake to adorn an otherwise simple façade.

Paxtang Avenue, Harrisburg, Dauphin County. This attractive Queen Anne home, built in the first decade of the twentieth century, is embellished through the use of Eastlake ornamentation.

Other Terms: Queen Anne Revival; Queen Anne/Eastlake
Years: 1870 – 1900

Gonder Mansion, Strasburg, Lancaster County. Benjamin Gonder constructed this ornate Queen Anne home in 1905 to serve as his summer house. The mansion is somewhat unique in the area in that its front façade is symmetrical.

The Queen Anne Style is the culmination of Victorian architecture and the quintessential style of the period. In fact, many people refer to a Queen Anne building simply as a "Victorian." Queen Anne was first popularized in England by architect Richard Norman Shaw, and then introduced to the United States in 1874 when architect H. H. Richardson designed the William Watts Sherman House in Newport, Rhode Island. The 1876 Philadelphia Centennial Exposition included several buildings designed in the Queen Anne Style and built by the British Commission, inspiring architects from throughout the country. *American Architect & Building News* further popularized the style.

Queen Anne was primarily a domestic style and was preferred by the wealthy. Homes in the style are lavish and highly decorated, and incorporate a variety of contrasting forms, materials, and rich colors.

Buildings are typically asymmetrical and feature steeply-pitched gabled roofs. Corner towers or turrets with conical roofs are a common feature. Chimneys are tall and reflect medieval inspiration, often featuring decorative pots or caps. Cross-gables and dormers are common. Bargeboards and finials further add to the vertical orientation of the style.

Façade materials include brick, wood siding, shingles and half timbers. Queen Anne homes typically feature brick or stone on the first level, with stucco, clapboard, or shingles on the upper stories. Half timbers may decorate the gabled ends of roofs.

Windows are frequently casement, and stained glass panels and transoms are common. Window sizes vary, and when multiple panes are present, the lower portion is typically a large single pane while the upper portion contains multiple smaller panes.

Porches and verandas are omnipresent, and frequently feature decorative details including Eastlake ornamentation.

Because Queen Anne is the quintessential Victorian style, there are many excellent examples to be found throughout South Central Pennsylvania. While the style is primarily for domestic architecture, there are several examples of commercial Queen Anne buildings including Lancaster's Southern Market House and Steinman Hardware Building. The William Wells Young School, in Wellsville, York County, is a fine example of a school designed in the Queen Anne style. Some of the magnificent homes in the style include Strasburg's Gonder Mansion, Columbia's Hermansader's Mansion, Middletown's Alfred's Victorian, and York's St. Clair House. The recently-restored Lady Linden in York is an excellent example of transitional Stick/Queen Anne, incorporating features from both styles and further augmented by Eastlake ornamentation.

Hermansader's Victorian Mansion, Columbia, Lancaster County. The home of artist Tom Hermansader was built in 1890 by Francis Bennett, who owned a dry goods business. In addition to the characteristic front-facing gable with decorative half-timbers and wraparound porch, the mansion features a corner tower with bell-shaped roof.

Farmers' Southern Market, Lancaster, Lancaster County. This ornate Queen Anne Style market house was constructed in 1888 from a design by C. Emlen Urban, Lancaster's most prominent architect. High relief bull and ram heads of terra cotta appear above the words Farmers and Market, respectively. The market, which cost $75,000 to build, was closed in 1986.

Lady Linden, York, York County. Built in 1887, the Lady Linden Bed & Breakfast is located northwest of York City in The Avenues. It was restored to its original grandeur beginning in 2006. The storybook home was constructed for Sam Nevin Hench and today exhibits four exterior colors that were present when the home was originally built. Lady Linden showcases the transition from Stick to Queen Anne as features from both styles are present, rounded out with Eastlake ornamentation.

St. Clair House, York, York County. This picturesque Queen Anne house was built by members of the prominent St. Clair family and was later the residence of the owner of Katz Brewing Company. The cross-gabled house features varying texture created by fish scale shingles, rubble, half timbering, and masonry.

High Victorian Gothic

Other Terms: Ruskinian Gothic; Late Gothic Revival
Years: 1860 – 1890

Mary Dixon Chapel, Lititz, Lancaster County. Linden Hall's Mary Dixon Chapel was built in 1882 in memory of a school graduate who died when she was only nineteen years of age. The polychromatic appearance is accomplished through contrasting bands of stone and red tile roof, with green and red paint for doors and window sills adding further color.

High Victorian Gothic is Gothic Revival with a Victorian "twist." Popularized by John Ruskin in his 1849 book, *The Seven Lamps of Architecture,* the style was primarily used for public buildings like libraries, municipal buildings, and churches. In contrast to the early Gothic Revival buildings in the United States, which drew from English inspiration, High Victorian Gothic buildings drew from the Gothic architecture of Continental Europe.

The two primary characteristics of a High Victorian Gothic building are pointed arches and a polychromatic, or at least dichromatic, appearance achieved through use of materials of varying colors and textures. Decorative bands, terra-cotta accents, and multicolored roof tiles all create the polychromatic look. High Victorian Gothic buildings are polychromatic because of the colors of the building materials and not necessarily the colors of the paint and stain.

Other features include arches or arcades, accented corners, and foliated or geometric carvings. High Victorian Gothic – like its counterpart, Victorian Romanesque – was an attempt to add the flair of the Victorian Era to a more traditional architectural style. Buildings are elaborate, massive, and "top-heavy"

– towers and large overhangs, as well as gables and dormers, create an emphasis on the rooflines. Heaviness is further stressed via deeply recessed windows. Exposed framing in gables is sometimes visible. In contrast to the heaviness of the style, spires – if present – are actually more slender than spires in the earlier Gothic Revival style.

Perhaps the most representative use of polychrome is the incorporation of two kinds of masonry, either through one color for walls and a second color for window arches, or brickwork banded with stone of a complimentary color.

There are several intriguing examples of this style in Central Pennsylvania. The Mary Dixon Chapel on the campus of Linden School in Lititz, Lancaster County, is an excellent example. Not only is the building polychromatic, but it also features alternating dark and light masonry bands on its façade. Grace Reformed Church in York also features a polychromatic appearance and varying textures, which include stone, wood, shingles, and tile. Two excellent examples can be found in Lebanon City, including St. Luke's Lutheran Church and Salem Evangelical Lutheran Church.

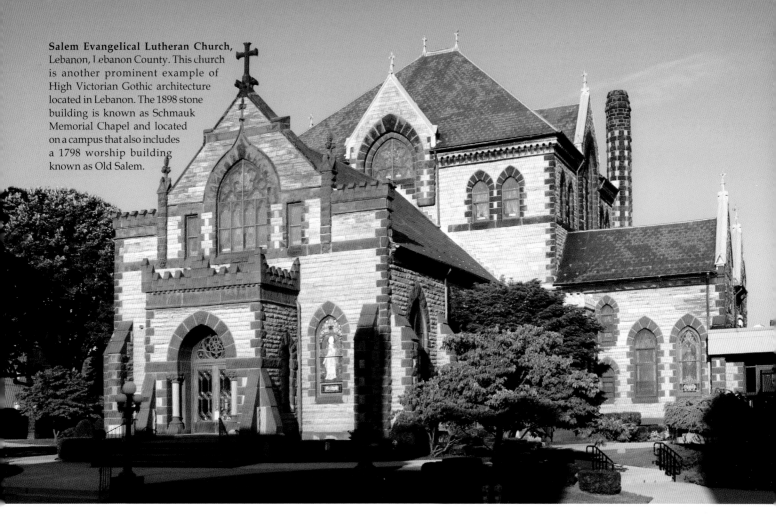

Salem Evangelical Lutheran Church, Lebanon, Lebanon County. This church is another prominent example of High Victorian Gothic architecture located in Lebanon. The 1898 stone building is known as Schmauk Memorial Chapel and located on a campus that also includes a 1798 worship building known as Old Salem.

St. Luke's Episcopal Church, Lebanon, Lebanon County. Henry Martyn Congdon, a New York City architect, designed this High Victorian Gothic Church in Lebanon 1879. The church was constructed of bluestone quarried adjacent to the building site.

Grace United Church of Christ, York, York County. This church, located in The Avenues neighborhood of York, contains varying colors and textures including white, gray, and brown stone, green shingles, red tiles, and exposed wood. The building was constructed in 1886.

Shingle

Other Terms: None
Years: 1880 – 1910

Schmidt House, York, York County. J.A. Dempwolf, York's most prolific architect, designed this mansion in 1889 for Anna and John C. Schmidt. The first floor is built of white granite in keeping with the common Shingle practice to utilize stone for the first story and shingles on the upper floors. The attractive building with Romanesque arches and Queen Anne influenced chimneys was restored in 2010.

First developed in New England for summer cottages, the Shingle Style replaced Queen Anne as the style of choice for houses and was popular around the turn of the twentieth century. Henry Hobson Richardson – best known for inspiring the Richardson Romanesque movement – was actually a major proponent of the Shingle Style, as was the firm of McKim, Mead and White. Architects drew from the Queen Anne and Colonial Revival Styles. The style is uniquely American and almost exclusively used for domestic architecture; in fact, early Frank Lloyd Wright designs are of this style.

The defining feature of a Shingle Style building is the uniform covering of wood shingles on the façade, frequently resulting in a monochromatic and flowing appearance. The exterior expression does not conform to a rigid style or formula, so the appearance of Shingle buildings greatly varies. Tones are typically warm in appearance, with the most common colors being gray, dark brown, and dark green.

Exposed foundations – and sometimes first stories – are of masonry or fieldstone. Buildings are most often horizontal in appearance, and the roof is a key visual element. Features include steeply pitched gambrel roofs, which may contain multiple planes, hipped or eyebrow dormers, towers, and massive chimneys. Wide, curved porches help give Shingle buildings their flowing form. In many examples, the lower plane of a gambrel roof serves as a porch roof. Roof cornices and porch posts are simple and unadorned. Entrances are plain.

Windows are usually double-hung and appear in groups of two or three. Leaded glass is common.

Locally, the Shingle Style did not enjoy the same popularity as other concurrent styles; however, examples can be found in late nineteenth and early twentieth century neighborhoods, particularly the "streetcar suburbs" built along trolley lines. Both the John Schmidt House and Charles Dempwolf House in York are Shingle Style homes built along a trolley line. Excellent examples can be found on South Front Street in Wrightsville and College Avenue in Elizabethtown. York's streetcar suburb, The Avenues, has several examples including a Shingle-Gothic church.

Trinity Lutheran Church, York, York County. Constructed around the turn of the twentieth century as the Chapel of the Holy Incarnation, this curious "Gothic-Shingle" building became home to Trinity Lutheran Church in 1913.

6
2

College Avenue, Elizabethtown, Lancaster County. Located on College Avenue in Elizabethtown, this charming Shingle Style home utilizes brick for its first floor. The red brick and dark brown shingles give the building its earthy tones. The interesting roofline includes front-facing gambrel with Palladian window, side-facing gable, and shed roof dormers.

Charles Dempwolf House, York, York County. Another Shingle-style home designed by J.A. Dempwolf, this time for his brother, who was president and director of several prominent companies and organizations.

St. James Episcopal Church, Lancaster, Lancaster County. Located on North Duke Street in downtown Lancaster, St. James Episcopal Church was originally constructed in 1820 and expanded multiple times between 1820 and 1880, when the building gained its current Romanesque Revival appearance.

Based upon round-arched medieval buildings, Romanesque Revival was most frequently used in ecclesiastical and institutional buildings. As with other Roman-influenced styles, the defining feature is the rounded or semi-circular arch. The Smithsonian Institute in Washington, D.C., which was designed by James Renwick, is one of the first and most famous examples of the style. Because Romanesque architecture was popular in Germany, architects from that country who immigrated to the United States practiced in that style, particularly for German Lutheran and Roman Catholic Churches.

Romanesque Revival buildings are typically monochromatic and built of brick or stone. Square or polygonal towers with pyramidal roofs are common. When employed for churches, one tower is often taller than the other(s). Romanesque Revival buildings characteristically incorporate an arcaded corbel table under the eaves as well as belt courses, which are defining features of the style. A wheel window is sometimes present, in addition to round-arched windows.

Wall surfaces are often smooth, particularly when compared to the massive, rough-cut façades of Richardson Romanesque. Victorian Romanesque buildings are technically Romanesque Revival; however, many architectural historians distinguish them as a sub-type or separate style because of their varied textures and dichromatic or polychromatic appearance.

Romanesque Revival was popular for churches throughout South Central Pennsylvania. Notable examples include Trinity United Church of Christ and First Presbyterian Church in downtown York, Saint James Episcopal Church and Lord's House of Prayer in Lancaster, and Zion Lutheran Church and Second Baptist Church in Harrisburg.

Second Baptist Church, Harrisburg, Dauphin County. This simple stone church, originally home to the Second English Church of Harrisburg, is located on Forster Street in Harrisburg. The church was constructed from 1863-1867 and maintains its original appearance with the exception of the tall steeple, which is no longer present.

First Presbyterian Church, York, York County. This Romanesque Revival church on East Market Street in York was constructed in 1861. The ornate façade contains hood molds, decorative corbels, engaged columns, and rosettes, among other decorative features. The church was designed by Philadelphia architect Joseph Hoxie, and built for $22,000. When originally constructed, the church was painted white.

Lord's House of Prayer, Lancaster, Lancaster County. Zion Lutheran Church was built in Lancaster in 1871, and the central tower was added in 1897. The congregation ceased operation in 1983 and today the East Vine Street building is home to the Lord's House of Prayer.

Richardson Romanesque

Other Terms: Richardsonian; Romanesque
Years: 1870 – 1900

Centre Presbyterian Church, New Park, York County. After graduating from The Cooper Union in New York, architect John A. Dempwolf relocated to Boston to superintend construction of the Cathedral of the Holy Cross. A few blocks away stood the recently-opened Trinity Church, the H.H. Richardson-designed building that launched an architectural style. The young Dempwolf was probably inspired by the building as several of his later designs, like Centre Presbyterian Church in New Park, reflect the style. The prominent Richardson Romanesque church was constructed in 1887-1888.

Only a handful of architects have been so influential that a style was named after them. Henry Hobson Richardson, the second American architect to study at the Parisian Écoles des Beaux Arts, is one of those architects. While he was a leading proponent of the Shingle Style, he also incorporated Romanesque Revival into simple, massive stone expressions. These bold buildings designed by Richardson – followed by scores of American architects influenced by him – incorporate Romanesque precedents, particularly the rounded arch. The style was mostly used for churches, schools, and public buildings, and Richardson's Trinity Church in Boston, which essentially created the style, is recognized as one of the ten most important buildings in the United States. Western Pennsylvania's Allegheny County Courthouse is another famous example.

The defining features of the style are rough-cut stone, massive arches, and monochromatic appearance. If there is one term that best defines the style, it is "heavy." Stone is usually gray granite or brownstone though brick and ashlar masonry are also used. Massive towers with conical roofs are common,

particularly on building corners. Slate or shingle roofs frequently feature eyebrow dormers and squat chimneys of stacked brick or stone.

Deeply recessed entrances are located under massive arches and often framed by short, sturdy columns. Double doors are commonly employed.

Windows are most often found in bands deeply recessed into the façade. Windows get smaller each successive story.

Local architects preferred the more refrained Romanesque Revival or the polychromatic Victorian Romanesque, which usually incorporated both brick and stone. The best example of Richardson Romanesque in South Central Pennsylvania is the Given Library in Mount Holly Springs, Cumberland County. Centre Presbyterian Church, a stone building located in New Park, York County, is also an excellent example of the style. The Historic Harrisburg Resource Center, as well as the 12th and 44th New York Infantry Monument on the Gettysburg Battlefield, also exhibit a Richardson influence. Middletown's Brownstone Café is a prominent example of the style.

Historic Harrisburg Resource Center, Harrisburg, Dauphin County. In 1894, the Central Guarantee Trust & Safe Deposit Company opened a new building shared with Merchants National Bank. The Hummelstown brownstone building with Indiana limestone base originally featured a hipped roof and rose window, which were removed in 1911.

Amelia S. Given Library, Mount Holly Springs, Cumberland County. James Steen, a Pittsburgh architect, designed this brownstone library in the Richardson Romanesque style in 1889. The attractive Mount Holly Springs library was constructed using Hummelstown Brownstone.

Brownstone Cafe, Middletown, Dauphin County. Completed in 1893 for the National Bank of Middletown, this brownstone Richardson Romanesque building was constructed by the firm of Hoshour, Dise and Company from Glen Rock, York County. The bank closed its doors three years later, and a series of banks occupied the building for the next century. Since 1998, a cafe has operated in the striking building.

Post Office & Federal Building, York, York County. This Victorian Romanesque building was designed as York's post office and home to Federal offices including the U.S. Revenue Department. It was built in 1895 from a design by Willoughby J. Edbrooke, Supervising Architect of the United States Treasury Department, the Federal agency tasked with the design of government buildings prior to the creation of the General Services Administration. Jeremiah O'Rourke, Edbrooke's successor, was most likely also involved with the project.

Unlike Romanesque Revival, which held true to Romanesque precedents, and Richardson Romanesque, which was monochromatic in appearance, the Victorian Romanesque Style was less formal and frequently dichromatic or polychromatic. As with other Romanesque influenced styles, the defining feature is the rounded arch. This style was primarily used for public and commercial buildings, and was more ornate than Richardson Romanesque. Some architectural historians include Victorian Romanesque within the Romanesque Revival category while others don't distinguish between Richardson Romanesque and Victorian Romanesque. Because of the inconsistency in the architectural community, Victorian Romanesque is broken out as its own style in this book.

Buildings in this style have different colors and textures, including rough-faced brick and stone, decorative terra cotta, and stone and brick trim. A brick building may feature stone trim, or vice versa

– this is one of the main differences with the more refrained Romanesque Revival, which typically features a formal, uniform façade.

Round arches are frequently supported on short, polished columns. Roofs and wall gables are steeply pitched, and towers are often topped with pyramidal or conical roofs. Gargoyles and grotesques are also common. Windows are arched and doors are set in rounded masonry arches. The arch is such a dominant form that first-floor arcades and ribbons of arched windows exemplify the style.

Victorian Romanesque was a favored style in South Central Pennsylvania, particularly for educational and public buildings. Examples include Biemesderfer Hall at Millersville University, Glatfelter Hall and Brua Chapel at Gettysburg College, Valentine Hall at Gettysburg Seminary, Lark Building at Lancaster Theological Seminary, and the old Post Office building in York. Both Lancaster and York's Central Markets are of the style.

Glatfelter Hall, Gettysburg, Adams County. Known originally as the New Recitation Building, this J.A. Dempwolf-designed building on the campus of Gettysburg College is now known as Glatfelter Hall. Dempwolf used red brick with accents of Hummelstown Brownstone and included a large central tower that reaches a height of 143 feet. Dempwolf designed a number of Gettysburg buildings in the Victorian Romanesque style, including the Brua Memorial Chapel at Gettysburg College and Valentine Hall at the Lutheran Theological Seminary at Gettysburg.

Biemesderfer Executive Center, Millersville, Lancaster County. Millersville University's 1895 library building is another fine example of Victorian Romanesque architecture. The architects for the project were P.A. Welsh and James H. Warner, the latter of whom is best known for designing the Lancaster Central Market.

Lark Building, Lancaster, Lancaster County. Located at the Lancaster Theological Seminary, the 1894 Lark Building was constructed of red brick and Hummelstown Brownstone. John Smith of Harrisburg designed the imposing building.

Market House is another type of building, and not a specific style. Many South Central Pennsylvania markets began as open air venues before moving into covered sheds or pavilions. Fortunately, quite a few of the region's historic farmer's market buildings are still used for their original purpose, while other market buildings have been rehabilitated and adaptively reused.

Though not housed in the oldest market building in the region, Lancaster Central Market does have the distinction of being the nation's oldest continually operating market. In 2009, it was named one of the Top Public Spaces in the United States by the American Planning Association. The Southern Market and Eastern Market buildings in Lancaster are also still standing and used for other purposes. Built in 1864, Harrisburg's Broad Street Market has the distinction of being the country's oldest continually-operated market house, a reference to the building itself. An Italianate Style market house was built adjacent to it a decade later. York's Central Market House and Market & Penn Farmers Market both still operate, while the buildings that once housed the Eastern Market and Carlisle Street Farmers Market are both still standing. The unique Columbia Market House in Lancaster County is once again operating as a farmers market. In Lebanon, the Market House that operated from 1892 until the 1960s is now operating again in its original home.

Broad Street Market, Harrisburg, Dauphin County. Harrisburg's Broad Street Market, originally known as the West Harrisburg Markethouse, is the last of six farmers markets that once operated in Harrisburg. Two buildings constitute the market: The older stone building opened in 1864 while its brick neighbor was completed in 1874 and expanded in 1877 and again in 1886.

Lebanon Farmers Market, Lebanon, Lebanon County. In 1892, Lebanon Farmers Market was constructed on the site that once housed the Lebanon County Jail, which had been destroyed by fire. The market operated until the 1960s. After a restoration project to the building, the farmers market was reborn, and is today again an important part of the Lebanon community.

Central Market, York, York County. Architect J.A. Dempwolf designed two prominent market houses in York. The first, a High Victorian Gothic building that was the home to York City Market House, was built in 1878 and demolished in 1963. The second, this building, was built in 1888 at a cost of $45,000. Baltimore shipwrights helped raise the roof of the structure, which was constructed by George Yinger.

Lancaster Central Market, Lancaster, Lancaster County. In addition to being recognized as one of the Top Public Spaces in the United States, Lancaster Central Market is also the anchor of Lancaster's vibrant downtown. The distinctive market with terra cotta roof was constructed in 1889 from a design by architect James Warner.

Columbia Market, Columbia, Lancaster County. Samuel Sloan and Isaac Hobbs designed the Columbia Market House, which was constructed in 1869. Other Lancaster County buildings designed by Sloan include the Lancaster County Courthouse and Fulton Opera House. Hobbs was best known as a creator of architectural pattern books, including *Authentic Victorian Villas and Cottages.*

Victorian Eclectic

Other Terms: Victorian; Late Victorian
Years: 1880 – 1900

Masonic Building, Gettysburg, Adams County. The most distinguishing feature of Gettysburg's Masonic Temple is the Flemish gable. The building was constructed in 1898.

Many Victorian Era buildings combine elements from a variety of styles and are not easily classified as one particular style. As pattern books became common in the mid-nineteenth century, builders and their clients would select favorite elements from different patterns – and styles – to be combined into a new building. The Philadelphia Centennial Exposition of 1876 introduced American architects to styles from throughout the world, inspiring them to incorporate exotic features into their Victorian designs. These two trends resulted in eclectic architectural combinations. Baltimore's iconic American Brewery, restored and now home to a non-profit organization, is the most famous example of the style.

There are several Victorian Eclectic buildings throughout the region. In some cases, they primarily fall under one style and are thus classified as that style, even though they combine features of multiple styles. In other cases, their appearance is distinctive, as is the case with the Central Hotel building in Mt. Joy, Masonic Building in Gettysburg, Stern Center in Carlisle, First National Bank building in Marietta, and both train stations in Lebanon City.

Central Hotel, Mount Joy, Lancaster County. The appearance of the eclectic Central Hotel in Mount Joy, part of Bube's Brewery, is the result of the original 1880 building and alterations made in 1893 after a fire. The original building was two stories with a mansard roof; after the fire, a full third story was constructed and a flat roof incorporated into the design.

Stern Center for Global Education, Carlisle, Cumberland County. When constructed in 1884, this Dickinson College building was known as the Tome Scientific Center. The building exhibits the rough-cut stone and eyebrow dormers of Richardson Romanesque, yet lacks the overall heaviness and massive arches of the style.

Cornwall & Lebanon Railroad Station, Lebanon, Lebanon County. This is one of two picturesque railroad stations located on North 8th Street in Lebanon. The other station was constructed for the Reading Railroad. This station, built for the Cornwall & Lebanon Railroad, was designed by brothers George Watson Hewitt and William Hewitt.

Chateauesque

Other Terms: French Chateau; Frances I
Years: 1880 – 1910

Milton Martin House, York, York County. Milton Martin, a York businessman who owned the Martin Carriage Works and willed a substantial sum of money to establish the library that bears his name, built his townhouse in 1900. J.A. Dempwolf was commissioned to design the home, as well as the adjacent Professional Building, which appears to the left of the Martin house in the photograph.

Inspired by the French chateaux of the sixteenth century, the Chateauesque Style was used to showcase wealth. Architect Richard Morris Hunt, the first American to study at the École des Beaux-Arts in Paris, popularized the style in America, though the first North American building in this style was built in Quebec, Canada. The Biltmore House, the largest residence in the country, was built for the Vanderbilt family and designed by Hunt in the Chateauesque Style. The style was not popular nationally, and the best stylistic examples are found in the northeastern United States.

Buildings in this style are asymmetrical and frequently imposing. The visual emphasis is on the roofline, which is steeply pitched and hipped, gabled, or mansard in form. Hipped roofs are either truncated or exaggerated to create large pyramidal shapes. Corner towers and turrets are typical, as are through-the-cornice dormers and parapets with curved or stepped gables. Pinnacles, spires, and tall decorative chimneys add further visual emphasis to the roof. Towers and turrets typically feature conical or candle-snuffer roofs.

Chateauesque buildings are almost always masonry, particularly stone. Windows and doorways feature semi-circular or basket handle arches, with hood molds and ogee arches over the windows. Shallow relief carving is sometimes present around doors and windows. Gothic stone tracery is also common in Chateauesque buildings. Belt courses provide ornamentation to façades as do corbels under balconies and turrets. Entrance canopies are characteristic.

Two notable examples of the style can be found in Lancaster, including the Peter Watt mansion, known as Roslyn, and the Hamilton Club, which was built for Catherine Haldeman Long. York's Milton Martin home and adjacent Professional Building are urban examples of the Chateauesque Style while the Colonial Hotel building on Continental Square is a large example that lost its distinctive roofline in a 1947 fire. The State Arsenal building in Harrisburg was designed in the style; however, much of the original building was demolished, and only the central tower remains, minus its original mansard roof. The Harrisburg Armory showcases the stylistic form, though it is not as elaborate as some of the other local examples.

Hamilton Club, Lancaster, Lancaster County. This prominent Chateauesque mansion was built in 1890 for Catherine Haldeman Long and later acquired by the Hamilton Club, a private social club named for the planner of Lancaster City, James Hamilton.

Roslyn, Lancaster Township, Lancaster County. Peter Watt, co-founder of the Watt & Shand Department Store, built this mansion west of Lancaster City in 1896. Designed by prominent architect C. Emlen Urban, it is one of the region's best examples of Chateauesque architecture.

Harrisburg Military Post, Harrisburg, Dauphin County. R. W. Shaw designed this building, also known as the Harrisburg Armory, in 1932. The simple Chateauesque building is located at the intersection of 14th and Calder Streets.

Neo-Norman

Other Terms: Castle-like; Romanesque
Years: 1870 – Early 1900s

Cumberland County Prison, Carlisle, Cumberland County. This structure, built in 1854, was designed by Edward Haviland, son of John Haviland. He designed a similar prison in York, which was later demolished. The brownstone used to construct the prison was quarried in York County.

Neo-Norman is sometimes used to refer to structures with a castle-like appearance. These buildings emulate the fortresses of the Norman period, which spanned from the mid-eleventh century through the mid-twelfth century. Norman architecture is technically Romanesque, and is characterized by massive structures built of unadorned masonry.

While originally used for castles, keeps, and other fortifications, as well as abbeys and cathedrals, the Neo-Norman interpretation of the style primarily refers to buildings that emulate castles. The style can also be thought of as a variation of the Richardson Romanesque style, because both incorporate heavy, rough-cut stone and massive arches. The defining feature of a Neo-Norman building, however, is the crenellation present along the roofline. Towers, turrets, and battlements are characteristic of the style.

While there aren't a lot of castles in South Central Pennsylvania, there are several buildings that were designed to emulate Norman architecture, including Lancaster County Prison in Lancaster, Cumberland County Prison in Carlisle, and Gethsemane Hall in York. The State Arsenal Building in Harrisburg is built of brick but otherwise exhibits the castle form.

Gethsemane Hall, York, York County. After the local Freemasons purchased the former York Post Office, they constructed this castle-like building on North Beaver Street to serve as their meeting hall.

Lancaster County Prison, Lancaster, Lancaster County. Architect John Haviland used a castle in Lancashire, England as inspiration for his design of the red sandstone Lancaster County Prison. When it was originally built, the $102,000 structure also contained a 110-foot central tower that served as an air shaft and stair tower. A famous prison architect best known for Philadelphia's Eastern State Penitentiary, Haviland's design for this prison was the final commission before his death in 1849.

Pennsylvania State Arsenal Building, Harrisburg, Dauphin County. When it was built in 1874, the Arsenal Building was two-stories in height and Chateauesque in style. A 1914 project entailed demolition of all but the prominent tower, and construction of a new castle-like three-story building. The tower is original, but no longer exhibits the mansard roof that once crowned it.

Renaissance Revival

Other Terms: Italian Renaissance
Years: 1870 – 1930

King Mansion, Harrisburg, Dauphin County. Frank Gordon Fahnestock, Jr. designed this palatial estate in 1926. The North Front Street building was built for local tax attorney Horace King and his wife, Rose. Designed in the Second Renaissance Revival style, the striking home cost an estimated $135,000 to build.

Renaissance Revival architecture, often referred to as Italian Renaissance, is sometimes viewed as a successor to Italianate and sometimes viewed as a subtype. The style essentially emulates the Renaissance Palazzi architecture of Northern Italy and was employed for imposing structures. Buildings constructed prior to 1890 are considered part of the "First Renaissance Revival," while post-1890 buildings are considered the "Second Renaissance Revival" and are typically larger than the earlier buildings. Some architectural historians prefer to use the phrase "Renaissance Revival," as the broad style includes French and even Spanish influences, not just Italian.

Renaissance Revival buildings have two personalities. For typical domestic architecture, buildings are usually symmetrical blocks and feature low hipped roofs, arched first-floor doors and windows, and smaller upper-story windows. Many contain full-width porches with heavy supports or projecting wings – either a central pavilion or smaller side wings.

High-style homes, as well as commercial and public buildings, have a somewhat different personality and appearance. While still symmetrical rectangles or squares, the imposing buildings frequently utilize moderately pitched roofs or flat roofs with balustrades and highly decorative cornices with dentils. Façades have distinct horizontal bands or divisions. Architects employed piano nobile, a technique that elevates visual emphasis above the ground; this was frequently accomplished via raised basements and first floors above the ground level. Pilasters and quoins further embellish façades. Ground floors may be rusticated and feature deeply recessed entrances and full-length, arched windows. Window treatments on upper floors are typically different from one-another, incorporating various styles, trim, and surrounds. Elaborate belt courses are also used to create distinct vertical bands. Small windows are found on the top or attic story.

Several of South Central Pennsylvania's most elaborate buildings were designed in the Renaissance Revival Style. Two prominent Harrisburg examples include the magnificent YMCA Central Branch Building, located at North and North Front streets, and the sprawling King Mansion, also on North Front Street. York's Capitol Theatre on North George Street showcases the style applied to a commercial building while Lancaster City Hall, originally a post office, exemplifies the style adapted for a public building. The Hershey Community Center, located in the heart of town, was built during The Great Depression, keeping the local workforce employed.

YMCA Central Branch Building, Harrisburg, Dauphin County. Designed by the architectural firm Lawrie and Green, this building was constructed in 1932. Lawrie and Green also designed the North Office Building on the Capitol Complex as well as the Dauphin County Courthouse. The inspiration for the design is said to be Santo Stefano's Basilica in Bologna, Italy.

Capitol Theatre, York, York County. The oldest section of the Strand-Capitol Performing Arts Center in downtown York was designed by Reinhardt Dempwolf, brother of J.A. Dempwolf. Reinhardt was trained at the École des Beaux-Arts in Paris and applied his training for the design of the Capitol Theatre, which was built originally as the one-story Theatorium in 1906, expanded in 1917 as The Jackson, then remodeled in 1926 as The Capitol. The adjacent Strand Theater, which has an elaborate Renaissance Revival interior, was designed E.C. Horn & Sons and opened in 1925.

Opposite page:
Hershey Community Center, Hershey, Dauphin County. This 190,000 square-foot limestone building was inspired by the architecture observed by Milton S. Hershey and his wife on their travels throughout Europe. The $3 million complex was built during The Great Depression, helping to keep the local construction tradesmen employed. Within the building is the 1900-seat, Venetian-style Hershey Community Theater.

Lancaster City Hall, Lancaster, Lancaster County. This Indiana Limestone building was designed by Philadelphia architect James H. Windrim. Completed in 1892, it has served as both a U.S. Post Office and Courthouse; in 1932, the building was repurposed as a city hall. Windrim served as Supervising Architect of the U.S. Treasury Department from 1889-1891.

Opposite page:
Saint Patrick Cathedral, Harrisburg, Dauphin County. This imposing church was built on State Street from 1904-1907. It employs a cruciform shape and a dome that reaches to 170-feet in height. Philadelphia's George I. Lovatt served as architect for the cathedral, which was constructed for a cost of $250,000. The exterior was totally restored in 2003-2005.

Colonial Revival

Other Terms: Georgian Revival; Federal Revival; Dutch Colonial Revival
Years: 1870 – 1920 (and beyond)

In 1877, architects Charles McKim and Stanford White toured New England during the summer months. Here they found inspiration in the architecture of Colonial America. Their designs that followed, coupled with the newfound patriotism born out of the Philadelphia Centennial Exposition of 1876, moved a generation of architects to design houses that reflected the nation's past. Colonial Revival is a broad category that includes Georgian Revival and Federal Revival. Originally, this style was very true to its Georgian precedent; however, as the style evolved, particularly with the mass marketing of pre-fabricated houses in the 1920s, Colonial Revival buildings became less formal. Buildings in this style tend to be larger than their Colonial counterparts, and features are more exaggerated. While there are many examples, both locally and beyond, of the style being used for commercial or institutional buildings, Colonial Revival was primarily a style of domestic architecture.

Most buildings in this style are rectangular in shape and feature a symmetrical façade, hipped or gabled roof with dentils or modillions providing a decorative touch. Truncated roofs feature widow's walks. Exterior materials are commonly beveled siding or brick. When clapboard is used, white, gray, and yellow are the most common colors; for brick buildings, red brick is the most popular, often laid in a Flemish bond and with light colored mortar.

Many Colonial Revival buildings feature a Neoclassical portico or pedimented entrance, and large porches are fairly typical, in contrast to the style's predecessors.

Windows are double hung and frequently grouped; splayed lintels and louvered shutters are also often present. A Palladian window above the front entrance is typical while entrances with fanlights and sidelights are also common. Higher style examples may feature pilasters or quoins as well as decorative swags and garland made of limestone.

Architects did maintain the central hallway as a key interior feature, incorporating the common floor plan of their inspiration. Today, simple Colonial Revival homes are extremely popular with developers – particularly as speculative homes – and are more accurately referred to as Neocolonial.

Colonial Revival was so popular that it spawned a "style" known as Dutch Colonial Revival, which is essentially a Colonial Revival building with a gambrel roof. Dutch Colonial Revival has its own variant, which features a wide, continuous dormer that creates a bungalow-type appearance. Additional characteristics of Dutch Colonial Revival include stepped dormers, wide overhanging eaves flared at the ends, and shutters with a decorative hole in the shape of a bell, pine tree, or half moon. A front-facing gambrel end is also common.

Colonial Revival was exceptionally popular in South Central Pennsylvania in the closing decades of the nineteenth century and throughout much of the twentieth century – long after the style had lost popularity elsewhere. Public buildings in the style include the Dauphin County Library in Harrisburg, YWCA of Lancaster, and York City Hall and Martin Library in York. As towns grew into cities, wealthy suburbs developed in the outer rings of the expanding towns, and it is in these neighborhoods where you'll find Colonial Revival homes. Springdale, south of downtown York, is an excellent example of this, with Colonial Revival being the single most popular style. Milton Hershey constructed his mansion in the style and the Pennsylvania Governor's Residence is also a notable example of Colonial Revival architecture – constructed several decades after the stylistic period ended.

Harrisburg Public Library, Harrisburg, Dauphin County. In 1914, this limestone Colonial Revival building was designed by James McCormick, Jr. and constructed on North Front Street at Walnut Street. The library became part of the Dauphin County Library System in 1976.

Stoll House, Harrisburg, Dauphin County. A Colonial Revival building with a gambrel roof is often referred to as "Dutch Colonial Revival." Designed by the architectural firm of Kast & Kelker, this North Front Street home was built in 1927 for Ernest A. Stoll.

Pennsylvania Governor's Residence, Harrisburg, Dauphin County. This $2 million Colonial Revival building was constructed to serve as the residence of the Governor of Pennsylvania and completed in 1968. The executive mansion was designed by Philadelphia architect George M. Ewing. Raymond Shafer, along with his wife Jane Davis Shafer, was the first governor to reside in the home.

Martin Library, York, York County. Frederick G. Dempwolf, son of J.A. Dempwolf, designed the Martin Memorial Library in York. The brick building, which features Indiana limestone accents, was constructed in 1935 for a cost of $100,000.

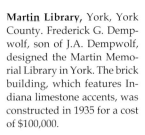

Gettysburg Post Office, Gettysburg, Adams County. James Knox Taylor also designed this Neoclassical building, which was completed in 1914. Today home to the Gettysburg Library, the building's architectural features include fluted columns with acanthus capitals and decorative Greek frets.

Planners of the 1893 World's Columbian Exposition in Chicago mandated that buildings have a classical theme. The resulting buildings, both large and small, created a wave of interest in Greek and Roman forms for public buildings and private homes. Architectural historians don't necessarily agree on the term for this style – the National Trust for Historic Preservation uses "Classical Revival," but most style guides use "Neo-Classical" or "Neoclassical Revival" to refer to the style that was popular throughout the first half of the twentieth century. From the 1880s into the 1920s, the country enjoyed a period known as the American Renaissance. Beaux-Arts is a term loosely applied to this period, with Italian Renaissance, Neoclassical Revival, and Beaux-Arts Classicism prominent styles of this movement. In fact, many architectural historians consider Neoclassical Revival to be the later, refined phase of Beaux-Arts. Amazingly, during the first two decades of the twentieth century, more marble was used in the United States than was used during the entire reign of the Roman Empire.

Neoclassical Revival buildings are generally larger than those of the earlier Greek Revival period and less ornate than those of Beaux-Arts Classicism. They are rectangular in shape and employ a formal symmetry. Buildings have a monumental appearance, usually in "temple" form. The defining feature is a full-height entry porch. Because of the concurrent popularity of the Colonial Revival style, many Neoclassical Revival houses are essentially Colonial Revival buildings with monumental classical porticos.

For houses, roofs are most often gabled or hipped, with front gables and side gables both being common. Massive public buildings are more likely to have flat roofs with balustrades. Cornices feature dentils or modillions. The full-height porches may span the width of the front façade or just the central portion. During the extended period of the style's popularity, columns evolved – at least with the domestic examples. The first half of the stylistic movement incorporated round, sometimes fluted, columns with classical capitals, the majority of which were Greek in design. However, during the latter years of the style's popularity, simple columns without capitals, frequently square in shape, began to replace their more elaborate predecessors.

Entrances are often intricate and incorporate designs from Georgian, Federal, and Greek Revival traditions.

Double-hung windows are rectangular in shape, rarely arched, and have lintels. Façades may include large expanses of space without fenestration or ornamentation. Neoclassical Revival buildings are constructed of masonry, including brick, marble, and smooth-faced limestone. The grandest of the domestic buildings and almost all of the public buildings use marble and limestone.

Neoclassical Revival buildings come in all shapes and sizes, and can be found in most South Central Pennsylvania communities. One of the larger examples is the North Office Building that is part of the Capitol Complex in Harrisburg. York's Post Office building is notable because it was designed by James Knox Taylor, Supervising Architect of the U.S. Treasury from 1897 to 1912. Under Knox's direction, hundreds of Federal buildings were executed in the Neoclassical Revival style. Taylor also designed Neoclassical Revival post offices in Hanover and Gettysburg. Breidenbaugh Hall, on the campus of Gettysburg College, is an example of a Colonial Revival building with a monumental Neoclassical portico. And Lower Grantley, a mansion south of York City, exemplifies how the Neoclassical Revival style was used to showcase wealth.

York Post Office, York, York County. Designed by James Knox Taylor, Supervising Architect of the U.S. Treasury, this marble building with granite base was constructed as a memorial to the Second Continental Congress and built in 1911. The appearance of today is the result of a $1 million expansion, completed in 1941.

Lower Grantley, Spring Garden Township, York County. The estate of George Small, known as Lower Grantley, was built in 1905 adjacent to Grantley, a mansion built by Small's parents. The Neoclassical Revival home features a colossal portico with Corinthian columns and a distinctive Palladian window.

North Office Building, Harrisburg, Dauphin County. The imposing granite and Indiana limestone building was designed by the firm of Gehron & Ross with Arnold Brunner originally serving as supervising architect. He died during the design phase, and the firm of Lawrie & Green took over. The 1929 building is a companion to the South Office Building.

Tudor Revival

Other Terms: Jacobean; Jacobethan Revival; Elizabethan Revival
Years: 1880 – 1940

McDevitt House, Elmwood Neighborhood, York County. This storybook false-thatched roof house emulates the famed Cotswold Cottages of rural England. It was designed by Russell Yessler and built for Harry J. McDevitt.

The quintessential Tudor Revival building features decorative half-timbering, yet roughly half of all Tudor Revival buildings contain no half timbers. In fact, the half timber building of which we are all so familiar is more accurately termed "Elizabethan Revival," as it is inspired by the English cottages built during the reign of Queen Elizabeth. The English Tudors, for whom the style is named, ruled from 1485 to 1558.

Tudor Revival buildings feature a steeply pitched roof, usually side-gabled, with one or more cross gables, steeply pitched triangular dormers, and tall, elaborate chimneys. Gables feature eaves of varying lengths, and some examples have a flared eave on one side only. Patterned brickwork or stonework is employed for chimneys, which are often topped with chimney pots.

Façades are of brick, stone, stucco, or wood, frequently with contrasting first and second stories. Decorative half timbering is a defining characteristic of the style, although it is not required. Stone trim is often employed and many examples have brick tabbing surrounding the front door.

Tall, narrow windows often appear in groups of three or four. Leaded windows with stone mullions are common as are round-headed or Tudor arches.

Tudor Revival was a very popular style in the early twentieth century. While perhaps not quite as prevalent locally as Colonial Revival, Tudor Revival homes can be found in the suburbs of the larger South Central Pennsylvania communities, standing alongside Colonial and Spanish Revival homes. Lancaster's School Lane Hills Historic District, west of the city, is brimming with Tudor Revival homes. Across the river in York, Springdale Historic District is another streetcar suburb with an abundance of Tudor Revival architecture. The Hahn House in Springdale reflects a Jacobean influence, though half-timbering is present on the rear of the home. The Civic Club building along North Front Street in Harrisburg is an excellent example of the half-timbering style while the Tracy Mansion showcases formal design without any half-timbering. One of the more interesting subtypes of Tudor Revival is the "false thatched roof," which is a rare variant of the style. York's Elmwood neighborhood features one of these storybook homes, designed to emulate England's Cotswold Cottages.

Tracy Mansion, Harrisburg, Dauphin County. When it was completed in 1918, the magnificent Tudor Revival mansion built for David Tracy boasted thirty rooms. The home was designed by prominent Harrisburg architect Charles Howard Lloyd and built by Central Construction Company.

Civic Club of Harrisburg, Harrisburg, Dauphin County. The Civic Club of Harrisburg is located in the former home of William and Virginia Fleming on Front Street. The building, which was constructed in 1902 and originally known as Overlook, was designed by William Hart Boughton. Upon her death, Virginia Fleming willed the house to the organization she co-founded, The Civic Club of Harrisburg. William W. Johnson designed a ballroom addition to the building in 1917.

Hahn House, York, York County. Nicknamed Crepler House when it was built by the Robert Emerton family, the imposing Hahn Home was designed by the J.A. Dempwolf architectural firm and built over the period of 1916-1918. The 18,000 square-foot mansion was built of rough-cut Pennsylvania quartzite and later became apartments and then a retirement home for women.

Old Main, Franklin & Marshall College, Lancaster, Lancaster County. The imposing Collegiate Gothic Recitation Hall, today known as Old Main, was designed by the Baltimore firm of Dixon, Balburnie and Dixon and completed in 1856. Two smaller buildings, Goethean Hall and Diagnothian Hall, stand to either side of the brick and sandstone building.

Late Gothic Revival flourished in the early 1900s and is considered to be the final period of the Gothic Revival, though the later buildings are frequently less elaborate than their predecessors. As with any Gothic structure, the defining feature is the pointed arch. Buildings are vertically-oriented and feature pointed-arch windows with tracery.

Façades are typically stone or brick, though tile was occasionally used. Decorative features include gargoyles and grotesques.

This style was most popular for churches; however, a secular version of the style became popular for higher education institutions and is known as Collegiate Gothic. Another offshoot of the style, which is commonly referred to as Neo-Gothic, was used for skyscrapers like the Woolworth Building in New York City and Tribune Tower in Chicago.

Many South Central Pennsylvania churches constructed in the early 1900s are Late Gothic Revival. Notable examples include Grace Lutheran Church and St. John's Lutheran Church, both in Lancaster, as well as Memorial Church of the Prince of Peace in Gettysburg and Memorial Lutheran Church in Harrisburg. York's Heidelberg Reformed (UCC) Church and Union Lutheran Church also exemplify the style. Franklin & Marshall's Old Main is perhaps the most famous local example of Collegiate Gothic architecture, and Lebanon Valley College's Old Main is another example of Gothic architecture applied to college campuses.

Humanities Building, Lebanon Valley College, Anville, Lebanon County.
The Administrative Building, today known as the Humanities Building,
was built in 1905 after a fire destroyed an earlier college building. It was
designed by architect Abner Ritcher, who incorporated Gothic and Tudor
influences into the landmark building.

Memorial Lutheran Church, Harrisburg, Dauphin County. In 1928, construction of this church, featuring stone quarried in Plymouth, Massachusetts, was finished. J.A. Dempwolf had completed the design for the building prior to his death in 1926.

Union Lutheran Church, York, York County. One of J.A. Dempwolf's final projects was Union Lutheran Church on West Market Street. The Gothic sanctuary was completed in 1927, one year after Dempwolf's death. Notably, the building features stained glass created by the Rudy Art Glass Studio.

School Lane Hills, Lancaster Township, Lancaster County. There are several fine examples of Spanish Colonial Revival architecture in the School Lane Hills historic district, including this late 1920s home on Wheatland Avenue.

While Mission and Spanish Colonial Revival are technically two different styles with their own unique features, the National Trust for Historic Preservation combines them into a single category.

The Mission Revival began in California and was popular in the Southwest, though architects throughout the country experimented with the style. As the name indicates, the style draws inspiration from the Spanish Missions of the American Southwest; however, Mission Revival structures are much simpler. The defining feature of the style is a curved parapet sometimes referred to as a "Mission parapet." Roofs are frequently hipped and tiled. Exposed rafters may extend beyond the wall, under the roof eaves. Buildings are stucco or plaster, with terra cotta ornamentation. Round arches and arcaded walkways are frequently present. Other features sometimes include a plain belt course and a tower, especially on larger buildings in the style.

In the early twentieth century, Spanish Colonial architecture saw a revival, not just in the Southwest but in suburban neighborhoods throughout the United States. Distinguishing features of the style include low-to-moderately pitched roofs, frequently hipped, and most often covered in red tile. Chimneys are capped with hoods. Walls are covered in stucco or plaster, though exposed masonry is not uncommon. When stucco is used, it is usually painted white, tan, yellow, or pink. Arches are commonly employed via arched windows and arcaded porches. Wrought iron grillwork is a recurrent feature for window grills and balconies. Doors are heavy and wooden. Higher style examples may include decorative relief, columns, window surrounds, multi-curved (Mission) parapets, and even bell towers. Larger examples of the style frequently feature courtyards.

While not nearly as common as its Colonial and Tudor Revival counterparts, Spanish Colonial Revival can be found throughout South Central Pennsylvania, particularly in the suburbs like School Lane Historic District in Lancaster, Springdale in York, and Uptown Harrisburg. The Elmwood Neighborhood in York features many examples, designed by a father and son team of architects, the Yesslers. Chocolate magnate Milton Hershey was enamored with Mediterranean architecture and chose to have his massive Hotel Hershey designed in the Mediterranean Revival Style. Mission Revival is uncommon in the region, though there are some modest examples with decorative mission parapets.

Eden House, Harrisburg, Dauphin County. Banker Alfred Eden and his wife, Jessie, lived in this attractive Front Street home, which was designed by Clayton J. Lappley and built in 1926 by William E. Bushey. A rear addition was constructed two years later.

Hotel Hershey, Hershey, Dauphin County. After vacationing in the Mediterranean region with his wife, Milton Hershey returned home with a postcard of a hotel where they stayed. He gave the postcard to his architect, D. Paul Witmer, as inspiration for a new hotel. Completed in 1933 at a cost of $2 million, the Mediterranean-influenced Hotel Hershey also includes twenty acres of formal gardens.

Yessler House, Elmwood Neighborhood, York County. Architect Russell B. Yessler designed this Yale Street home for himself and his Cuban-born wife. Yessler, along with his father Harry Yessler, designed much of the Elmwood neighborhood and brought the Spanish Colonial Revival style to York.

Beaux-Arts Classicism

Other Terms: Beaux-Arts
Years: 1880 – 1920

The École des Beaux-Arts was founded by Louis XIV to train architects specifically to work on his Palace at Versailles. In the early nineteenth century, Napoleon reestablished the school, which trained a generation of architects in the classical orders. Architectural icons Richard Morris Hunt and H.H. Richardson were the first two American architects to train at the school. They paved a trail that was followed by countless architects, as a year spent abroad at École des Beaux-Arts became almost a rite of passage. Beaux-Arts is both a period in American architecture, sometimes known as the American Renaissance, and a style of architecture, commonly referred to as Beaux-Arts Classicism. As a period, Beaux-Arts includes Renaissance Revival (Italian Renaissance), Neoclassical Revival, and Beaux-Arts Classicism. As a style, it is grandiose, free-form interpretation of the classical orders. Beaux-Arts buildings showcase Gilded Age prosperity, personal and corporate wealth, and civic pride. Expositions in Philadelphia (1876), Chicago (1893), and St. Louis (1904) featured grand Beaux-Arts buildings, inspiring visiting architects to return home and begin emulating the style.

Elaborate and even pretentious are terms frequently used to describe buildings in this style. Beaux-Arts buildings are most often symmetrical and monumental in appearance. Their design is less formal than the contemporaneous Neoclassical Revival, even though architects borrowed from the same historic sources. Roofs are flat and have parapets or classical balustrades, though an urban subtype of the style often features a slate-covered mansard roof with stone dormers. Chimneys, if present, are minor in scale and sometimes built in pairs. Grand domes may be present, and statuary frequently adorns the roofline. Ornamented cornices further embellish the appearance.

Heavy ashlar stone provides for strong foundations while façades almost always comprise stone material, particularly white marble and beige limestone, though red brick and even stucco-clad examples do exist. Beaux-Arts buildings are heavily ornamented, and architects accomplished this through use of columns, pilasters, quoins, wreaths, swags, cartouches, and statuary – sometimes all on the same building. Windows also receive a highly decorative treatment. Both arched and rectangular windows are employed, with stone surrounds, pediments, lintels, and pilasters adding to the overall heaviness of the appearance.

The main entrance is typically centered on the front elevation, and framed by columns, pilasters, and arched openings. One of the defining characteristics of Beaux-Arts Classicism is the presence of paired columns and pilasters. This provides a way to differentiate the style from Neoclassical Revival, which incorporates single columns and pilasters. Both Roman and Greek orders are employed, and grand stairways are common.

South Central Pennsylvania has many excellent examples of Beaux-Arts Classicism, with none better recognized than the Pennsylvania Capitol Building. The adjacent Matthew Ryan Legislative Office Building is another excellent example of the style. Lancaster's Watt & Shand building on Penn Square, which is essentially a preserved façade with modern hotel behind it, showcases how the style was adopted for commercial use. The Pennsylvania Monument on the Gettysburg Battlefield is the largest monument in the National Park and reflects the Beaux-Arts Classicism style. In York, the First National Bank building on Continental Square and York Gas Company building on West Market Street showcase the ornate style. Lebanon Valley College's Carnegie Library is another local example.

Speaker Matthew J. Ryan Legislative Office Building, Harrisburg,
Dauphin County. Known originally as the Executive, Library, and Museum
Building, this 1894 limestone building is the oldest on Capitol Hill and was
designed by architect John Torrey Windrim.

Pennsylvania Monument, Gettysburg, Adams County. The largest monument on the Gettysburg Battlefield is the Pennsylvania Monument, which was built in 1910 at a cost of $182,000. W. Liance Cottrell submitted the winning design, out of more than fifty entrants, in a contest to design the new monument. More than 1,250 tons of granite and 22 tons of marble were used to construct the memorial.

Watt & Shand Building, Lancaster, Lancaster County. The original portion of the Watt & Shand Department Store building was designed by C. Emlen Urban and built on Penn Square in 1898. Several subsequent additions were constructed while existing buildings connected on the interior were refurbished with a Beaux-Arts façade to match the original Urban building. Today, the façade is all that remains, thanks to a façade-ectomy that entailed demolition of the entire complex and construction of a new hotel and convention center.

Pennsylvania Capitol Building, Harrisburg, Dauphin County. Philadelphia architect Joseph Huston designed this National Historic Landmark, which comprises five horizontal and five vertical sections. The Vermont granite building employs heavy use of Greek and Roman motifs, and is topped by a dome directly inspired by the dome on Saint Peters Basilica in Rome. The grand staircase was adopted from Garnier's Paris Opera House.

French Eclectic

Other Terms: French Revival; French Rural
Years: 1915 – 1950

French Eclectic is a residential style, incorporating elements from earlier French influenced styles: Beaux-Arts Classicism, Chateauesque, and Second Empire. French Eclectic buildings have their own identity and capture the beauty of rural France. The style was most popular in the 1920s and 1930s, as World War I soldiers returned home, inspired by the architecture they had observed in France. A resurgence of the style began in the 1960s. Notably, the French Eclectic style shares many similarities with Tudor Revival because countless examples in northern France were built in the Medieval English tradition.

The most common type of French Eclectic home features a formal, symmetrical façade with steeply-pitched hipped roof. Less formal examples are asymmetrical, and contain off-center doorways. A predominant subtype exhibits a circular tower with conical roof. Most often, the tower is nested in the corner of an "L" shaped building, and the main entrance is located in the base of the tower.

Exteriors are of brick, stone, or stucco. Decorative half-timbering, quoins, and random bricks or stones accent the façade. In these examples, roofs are still steeply pitched, though they may be hipped or gabled. Shingles or tiles are employed for French Eclectic roofs.

Hipped, arched, or gabled dormers break the cornice line, and upper story windows also sometimes break the roofline. Chimneys are sizeable and eaves are sometimes flared.

Entry doors frequently have a stone or terra-cotta surround, normally in arched openings, and French doors are also popular within the style.

Windows are varied, with examples featuring double hung, casement, and full-length casement.

While this style is not nearly as common as Colonial and Tudor Revival, a few examples can be found in the region's early twentieth century neighborhoods, including York's Springdale neighborhood and Lancaster's School Lane Hills historic district. An excellent example of the hipped roof formal style is located on Manor Street in Harrisburg, while two storybook examples of the asymmetrical subtype can be found on Front Street and in the Bellevue Park neighborhood.

Schmidt House, York, York County. Horace Schmidt, secretary of Schmidt & Ault Paper Co., constructed this home in 1929; exemplary features include a steeply-pitched gable roof, corner tower with entrance, random stones, and door tabs.

School Lane Hills, Lancaster Township, Lancaster County. Because French Eclectic houses frequently feature decorative half-timbering, some people mistakenly refer to them as Tudor Revival. Though it contains half-timbering, this late 1920s home on Wheatland Avenue is textbook French Eclectic with corner entrance tower, random stone accents, flared eaves, and through-the-cornice dormers.

Eby House, Harrisburg, Dauphin County. This stately home was built in 1930 for S.R. Eby, an attorney. The architect for the Manor Street home was M. Edwin Green and the builder was Richard Lawrie, Jr.

Norman Towers, Harrisburg, Dauphin County. The Lewis and Maude Troup House, or Norman Towers, was built in 1929 for a cost of $75,000. The unique design features two towers, one facing Front Street and a second facing River Road. Edmund Good, Jr. was the project architect.

Prairie

Other Terms: American Foursquare
Years: 1900 – 1930

Green Street, Harrisburg, Dauphin County. This rambling Prairie Style home was built in the 1940s on Green Street near Italian Lake.

Inspired to create a new American style, Frank Lloyd Wright pioneered the Prairie Style, which was primarily used for domestic buildings. The term "prairie" does not come from Wright, but from a 1901 *Ladies Home Journal* article that featured one of his designs with the caption, "A small house in a prairie town." The Prairie Style can be considered early experimentation with the organic architecture for which Wright became famous as he set out to create a design that reflected the Midwestern prairie terrains. The style was most popular in the Chicago area, though examples exist throughout the United States.

A typical Prairie house is two stories with a one-story wing, porch, or porte-cochére. Homes are built of brick or timber, but are frequently covered in light-colored stucco with dark accents. Buildings have an undeniable horizontal orientation, due to the walls and terraces that extend from the main structure as well as low-pitched hipped roofs with large overhanging eaves. Long bands or ribbons of windows further emphasize the horizontal focus. Windows are usually casement with small panes of glass. While roofs are unadorned, a massive central chimney is often present.

Main entrances frequently do not front the street; rather, they are almost hidden from sight. Glazed doors feature geometric decorative patterns.

A simplified version of this style is known as the American Foursquare and was popularized by mail-order catalogues like that of Sears, Roebuck, Company. A typical American Foursquare may be brick or wood and is two stories with a one-story porch. While it is a very simple version of Prairie, it far exceeded its inspiration in popularity.

While there are several fine examples of the Prairie Style in South Central Pennsylvania, the American Foursquare interpretation is far more common. The most interesting example of Prairie Style is located near New Cumberland and was designed by a protégé of Frank Lloyd Wright. Examples can also be found in early twentieth century neighborhoods in York, Lancaster, and Harrisburg. The Foursquare style, in contrast, is omnipresent in almost every community in the region as it was inexpensive to build and favored by developers during the time period.

North 17th Street, Harrisburg, Dauphin County. Harry Brewster Shoop designed this home in 1911 for George Shreiner, a developer and builder of the surrounding neighborhood. Shreiner lived in the Prairie Style house for several years.

Old York Road, New Cumberland, York County. Though the Prairie Style is associated with the early twentieth century, architects continued to design Prairie homes well after the style was no longer in vogue. Bill Parks, an architect and Frank Lloyd Wright protégé, designed this York Road house in 1970.

South George Street, York, York County. This building is an example of the simplified vernacular version of the Prairie Style known as American Foursquare. Most examples aren't this elaborate in terms of architectural detailing, but share a similar form.

Commercial

Other Terms: Chicago School; 20th Century Commercial
Years: 1875 – 1930

Hager Building, Lancaster, Lancaster County. Lancaster's steel and terra cotta Hager Building was designed by C. Elman Urban and built in 1911 to serve as the Hager Department Store. Urban enriched the skeletal appearance with Beaux-Arts styled ornamentation.

Opposite page:
Dauphin County Veterans Memorial Office Building, Harrisburg, Dauphin County. Formerly known as both the Blackstone Building and the Claster Building, this eight-story brick and limestone building was designed by architect Charles Howard Lloyd and completed in 1920. The building was constructed by local merchant Henry Claster and occupied by the Pennsylvania Public Services Commission.

A small group of architects working in Chicago are often credited with pioneering this style, though latter day architectural historians have noted that buildings in New York City and Philadelphia pre-dated the most famous examples in Chicago. Louis Sullivan was the best known practitioner of the style, and his buildings featured a tripartite scheme that included base (street level), shaft (middle floors), and capital (top floor and decorated terra-cotta cornice). William LeBaron Jenney, who designed the First Leiter Building in Chicago, was one of the earlier pioneers. Many style guides identify Commercial Style buildings as being six to twenty stories; however, there are plenty of examples less than five stories.

Sometimes referred to as the Chicago School, this style was popular for department stores and large office buildings. Features include large rectangular windows, projecting bay windows, flat roofs, liberal use of terra cotta, and a sometimes-skeletal appearance due to the large expanse of glass and narrow expanse of brick or terra cotta. From this style comes the "Chicago window," which features a large central pane flanked by two slender panes. The use of skeletons of iron and steel allowed buildings of great height.

Chicago architect Louis Sullivan began to add his own type of ornamentation, which was later copied and is commonly referred to as Sullivanesque. Because Commercial Style buildings were typically massive, plain buildings, architects tended to incorporate features from other styles to embellish the façades.

The Bon-Ton Building in York, which was constructed in 1911 as a department store, is the area's best example of the style. The Bear's Department Store, built on nearby Continental Square during the same period, also draws influence from the Commercial Style, though it incorporates features from other styles as well. Several examples in Harrisburg have been torn down over the years, though a number of façades of Commercial Style buildings were incorporated into Strawberry Square. Dauphin County Veteran's Memorial Office Building is another Harrisburg example while the Hager Building is Lancaster's best example of the style.

Bear's Department Store, York, York County. During downtown York's heyday as a center for retail, Bear's Department Store, on Continental Square, was a major destination for shoppers. The building was designed by J.A. Dempwolf in the Commercial Style, though Italianate-style brackets were used to enhance the building's overall aesthetic.

Bon-Ton Store, York, York County. Once the flagship store of The Bon-Ton department store chain, this building was designed by J.A. Dempwolf and constructed in 1911. Dempwolf designed the building around massive Chicago windows and embellished its skeletal appearance with white tile and stepped parapets, adding visual emphasis to the roofline. Today the building houses York County Government offices.

"Craftsman" is a style of building while "bungalow" is a type of building. A building can be designed in Craftsman style but yet not be a bungalow. Likewise, a bungalow can be designed in an architectural style other than Craftsman. However, the National Trust for Historic Preservation, and many architectural historians for that matter, combine them into a master category because the archetypal bungalow has Craftsman features.

The Craftsman Style had its beginnings in England by architects John Ruskin and William Morris. In the United States, Gustav Stickley's magazine, *The Craftsman*, showcased the movement throughout the country. His design for the New Jersey community known as Craftsman Farms is the most famous community in the style. The overall appearance of a Craftsman building is rustic or natural. Wood, stone, and brick are common façade materials and the overall color palette is earth-toned, including browns, olives, and terra-cotta reds. Masonry first floors and wood, shingle, or stucco second floors are typical, as are fieldstone foundations. Roofs are most often gabled and feature wide eaves, and porches are also front-gabled. Exposed rafters and overhanging wood beams are defining features of the style.

The overall design is asymmetrical, though when used on bungalows symmetry is common. Square or tapered (battered) columns, heavy casement windows, and battened doors with wrought iron hinges are also common elements. Heavy front doors often feature glass in the upper third and sidelights may also be present. Not only do Craftsman buildings depict a rustic, simpler time, but they also emphasize structural elements like rafters, joints, hinges, and pegs. Sears, Roebuck, Company featured several models of Craftsman homes in their mail-order catalog.

The term "Bungalow" is used to refer to a variety of buildings – any small home, buildings of one or one-and-a-half stories, or Craftsman homes. A true Bungalow, or Bungaloid, has roots in the Arts & Crafts Movement. The popularity of the Bungalow was driven by the need for simple, low cost homes. In California, Bungalows were built with Craftsman features including battered porch piers, cobblestone chimneys, and exposed roof rafters. As Bungalows became popular across the country, architects incorporated features from Japanese architecture, Prairie, Spanish Colonial Revival, Stick, and even Swiss Chalets. A "typical" Bungalow, if there is such a thing, is one or one-and-a half story (the "half" story being a livable attic with small window or dormer) and has a front-facing gabled roof with either a small gabled dormer or a smaller gabled roof over the front porch. A large porch is a very common feature of a Bungalow, no matter what the stylistic influence. Sears, Roebuck, Company published mail-order catalogues featuring Bungalows with pre-cut boards and materials, ready for assembly, resulting in inexpensive Bungalows being constructed throughout the country.

In the region, there are not many Craftsman-style buildings that aren't also Bungalows; however, Bungalows – Craftsman and other styles – are prevalent throughout South Central Pennsylvania. They are as natural in early twentieth-century neighborhoods as they are on rural roads. Some towns, like Elizabethtown, have a high concentration of bungalows. One of the most unique Craftsman style buildings in the country is Indian Steps Museum in Airville, which features all the characteristic details of the Craftsman style, then adds hundreds of Native American artifacts in the walls of the building. Excellent examples of Craftsman/Bungalows are found in the Springdale neighborhood of York City and on East Chocolate Avenue in Hershey. The former example is constructed of brick while the latter example is built of stone. A row of simple bungalows purchased from Sears, Roebuck can be found on the Lincoln Highway near Thomasville while Uptown Harrisburg has several excellent examples.

Springdale Neighborhood, York, York County. This is one of several Craftsman/Bungalows in and around the Springdale neighborhood of York City. The textbook home incorporates a large porch, battered columns, and exposed rafters.

Indian Steps Museum, Airville, York County. A high style and very unique example of Craftsman architecture is the former home of John Edward Vandersloot, today the Indian Steps Museum of the Conservation Society of York County. Thousands of Native American artifacts collected by Vandersloot adorn the walls of the handsome building – both inside and out. This building is too big to be a Bungalow, yet exhibits Craftsman features like a fieldstone first floor, exposed brackets, earth tones, battered columns, and battened doors.

East Chocolate Avenue, Hershey, Dauphin County. Constructed in 1911, this Craftsman/Bungalow is built of stone. Among the exemplary features of the home are front-facing gables, exposed rafters, and wide eaves.

Academy Manor Neighborhood, Harrisburg, Dauphin County. These two Craftsman/Bungalows are located on North Second Street near the Academy Manor neighborhood.

Modern Movements

Art Deco

Other Terms: Deco
Years: 1925 – 1940

Catherine Hall, Hershey, Dauphin County. Chocolate magnate Milton S. Hershey had a hand in the design of the iconic Catherine Hall building, which has stood over Hershey since its construction in the 1930s. The Art Deco building was one of several major construction projects undertaken by Milton Hershey during the Great Depression as a way to keep the local community employed. In 2007, the rear portions of the building were demolished and rebuilt as a modern middle school for the Milton Hershey School; however, the historic Art Deco front portion of the building was maintained and restored.

Art Deco was popular in the 1920s and 1930s, particularly for movie houses and other public buildings. The style is named for the Exposition Internationale des Arts Dècoratifs et Industriels Modernes, or International Exposition of Modern Industrial and Decorative Arts, held in Paris in 1925. Event organizers required a focus on the future, even prohibiting "reproductions, imitations, and counterfeits of ancient styles" for participants. "Art Deco" essentially refers to a type of decoration that relies on stylized geometry and ornamentation. Furniture, jewelry, and even clothing can also be classified as Art Deco.

Architects who designed in the style rejected the revivalist traditions popular at the time. Common features of buildings in the style include a vertical emphasis and a series of set-backs on the façade. Exteriors are built of concrete or smooth stone, terra cotta is used for accents, and colors are often vivid.

Low relief ornamentation of floral and fountains frequently surrounds doorways and windows and also appears on parapets and roof edges. Windows are usually straight-headed and frequently appear in bands. Buildings of this style generally have an angular or hard edge composition, which differentiates Art Deco from Art Moderne, a streamlined style that was originally lumped under the Deco heading.

There are many excellent examples of Art Deco buildings in the region. Some of the best and largest examples can be found in Harrisburg, including the Fulton Bank Building (originally the Harrisburg Hotel), Payne-Shoemaker Building, Dauphin County Courthouse, and Northwest Office Building of the Capitol Complex. Lancaster's best-known Art Deco buildings are Shaub's Shoe Store and the Steinman Building, home to Lancaster Newspapers. York Hospital's original building, constructed in 1929, is probably York County's largest example of the style. The York Telephone & Telegraph Building in downtown York is notable, as is the Hanover Shoe building on the square in Hanover. In Hershey, both the former Hershey Chocolate factory as well as Catherine Hall of the Milton Hershey School exemplify the style.

Payne Shoemaker Building, Harrisburg, Dauphin County. Contractor Ray Shoemaker and developer Frank Payne partnered to build the appropriately-named Payne Shoemaker Building, which was completed in 1930. The thirteen-story tower is located on North Third Street and was designed by Clayton Lappley.

Dauphin County Courthouse, Harrisburg, Dauphin County. "Modern Classic" is the term that architects at Lawrie and Green used to refer to the county courthouse when it was constructed, but it is recognizable as an Art Deco building. The Georgia marble building is notable for its many engravings and inscriptions, both inside and out.

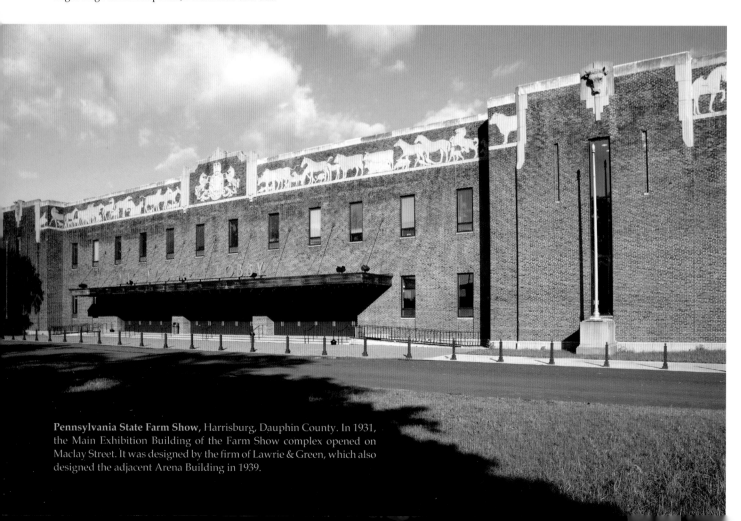

Pennsylvania State Farm Show, Harrisburg, Dauphin County. In 1931, the Main Exhibition Building of the Farm Show complex opened on Maclay Street. It was designed by the firm of Lawrie & Green, which also designed the adjacent Arena Building in 1939.

TE Connectivity, Harrisburg, Dauphin County. One of the most interesting Art Moderne buildings in South Central Pennsylvania, this structure became part of Amp Incorporated (later Tyco Electronics and now TE Connectivity) in 1951.

A distinctive "streamline" appearance is the dominant feature of Art Moderne, which was popular in the 1930s and 1940s. To many architectural historians, "Art Moderne" is merely an extension of the Art Deco movement. When broken out into a separate style, Moderne is defined by curves while Deco is defined by angles and hard edges; Moderne is horizontal while Deco is vertical. Legendary architect Frank Lloyd Wright actually designed one of the greatest buildings in the style, the administration building for Johnson Wax in Racine, Wisconsin. Perhaps the best known application of Art Moderne was the Pan Pacific Auditorium in Los Angeles, which burned in 1984 but was the inspiration for the entrance to Disney's Hollywood Studios and Disney's California Adventure.

In some ways, Art Moderne – or Streamline, a term many historians use – was a celebration of transportation engineering, drawing inspiration from cars, trains, and even ships. Common features include rounded corners, smooth surfaces, flat roofs, minimal ornamentation, and glass plate windows in horizontal bands. Curved window glass, glass block, cement panels, stainless steel doors, and window trim are all hallmarks of Art Moderne buildings. When built of brick or concrete, walls are often covered in plaster.

Unlike Art Deco's frequent inclusion of low relief ornamentation, Art Moderne buildings typically feature no ornamentation other than a stringcourse. When nautically-inspired, buildings contain pipe railings on balconies and stairs as well as round windows.

Nationally, as well as locally, Art Moderne was not as popular as Art Deco. Harrisburg's Polyclinic Hospital exhibits features of the style, but the TE Connectivity building on Paxton Street and PennDOT building on Route 22 are better examples. Ephrata is home to Royer's Pharmacy, a noteworthy streamlined building. York is home to two similarly-named buildings, both in the style: the White Rose Motor Club building on East Market Street and White Rose Motor Company on West King Street. The Modernaire Motel east of York City is a great example of the architecture that sprung up along the Lincoln Highway. More prevalent than permanent buildings in the style are the myriad prefabricated Art Moderne diners that are found throughout South Central Pennsylvania.

Modernaire Hotel, York, York County. Located east of York City, the appropriately-named Modernaire Hotel is a throwback to the heyday of the Lincoln Highway. Note the curved wall and glass blocks, hallmarks of the style.

Royer's Pharmacy, Ephrata, Lancaster County. This Art Moderne building, which dates from the late 1930s, is located on Main Street in the heart of Ephrata. Like many examples of the style, the entrance is located in the rounded building corner. The stainless steel on the front façade and signage are textbook Art Moderne.

White Rose Motor Club, York, County. This building in downtown York was constructed in 1949 and features curved glass and stainless steel. The streamlined appearance of Art Moderne proved to be a perfect fit for an automobile club.

James Minick House, Camp Hill, Cumberland County. James Minick, a mid-twentieth century architect, designed this house for himself and wife Leah. Located on Cumberland Boulevard, the International Style house was completed in 1941 and featured in *Architectural Record* magazine in 1944.

The International Style, which began in Europe in the 1920s, is based around a skeletal frame with exterior skin that comprises clerestory windows and smooth wall panels. Windows are often in bands, and turn corners. Walter Gropius and Mies Van Der Rohe were German architects and international leaders in the style, as was French architect Le Corbusier. In 1928, Richard Neutra introduced the style to the United States with his design of the Lovell "Health" House in Los Angeles. The Museum of Modern Art in New York City, which featured a 1932 exposition on modern architecture, is credited with coining the term "International Style."

The style is devoid of ornamentation and uses modern construction materials. Typically rectangular or square, an International Style building has a flat roof with no eaves, projecting or cantilevered balconies on upper floors, and glass curtain walls. In fact, the International Style is an expression of a building's structure as much as it is an expression of an architectural style. Buildings have a horizontal or linear orientation, though the style was also popular for glistening skyscrapers. Architects practicing in the style rejected the ornamentation of Art Deco and period revivals.

One of the most famous architects of the International Style, Louis Kahn, designed a notable building in Harrisburg, the Olivetti-Underwood factory in Colonial Park. Other examples include the Pennsylvania Labor & Industry Building and Ronald Reagan Federal Building, both in Harrisburg, as well as the James Minick House in Camp Hill. Harrisburg's 25-story Pennsylvania Place apartment building is another noteworthy example.

Ronald Reagan Federal Building and Courthouse, Harrisburg, Dauphin County. This 12-story building is constructed of glass curtain wall and steel. It was completed in 1966 and is owned by the General Services Administration (GSA).

Pennsylvania Department of Labor & Industry, Harrisburg, Dauphin County. Lacey, Atherton & Davis, an architectural practice based in Wilkes-Barre, designed this 18-story building. Completed in 1954 at a cost of $9 million, the building features gray Indiana limestone and Georgia marble. John McShain Construction of Philadelphia served as contractor for the project.

Olivetti-Underwood, Harrisburg, Dauphin County. While world-renown architects, sometimes called "starchitects," don't usually design industrial buildings, a notable local exception is this building along Interstate 81, which was designed by Philadelphia-based architect Louis Kahn.

During the twentieth century, American architecture ceased conforming to the standards of a given style like Georgian or Italianate, as architects began experimenting with classical styles and new forms, modern materials, and new trends in design. The idea of a "style" became difficult to characterize, and many architectural historians today shy away from applying stylistic labels to buildings. In some cases, like Wrightian, architects mimicked another architect – in this case, Frank Lloyd Wright – and a label was created to qualify these new buildings. However, the overarching term "Modern" is perhaps most appropriate. Walter Gropius, a famous twentieth century architect, compared style labels of contemporary architecture to coffins, noting that all that labels do is create confusion.

Even so, there are some stylistic labels recognized by architectural historians. These include:

New Formalism, a style which entails free standing symmetrical blocks. Buildings are top-heavy, with flat projecting rooflines. Walls are smooth and even glossy. Arches are common. Ornamentation is achieved through patterned screens or grills. Philip Johnson is the best known practitioner of the style, and his design of the Amon Carter Museum in Fort Worth, Texas, is perhaps the most famous example.

Wrightian is a term applied both to buildings inspired by Frank Lloyd Wright as well as buildings designed by Wright during the second half of his career. The most famous examples include Fallingwater in Western Pennsylvania and the Guggenheim Museum in New York City.

Neo-Expressionism refers to buildings with sweeping curves, particularly in rooflines and walls. Geometrical forms are used minimally, and concave and convex shapes are common. Spaces are arched or vaulted. Neo-Expressionism is characterized by an avoidance of rectangular shapes. Dulles International Airport is the most famous example of this style.

Brutalism is defined by weight and mass. Buildings are rectangular and usually feature a flat roof. Windows are treated like holes in walls. Exposed rough concrete is the defining characteristic, both for broad expanses of wall as well as structural framework. However, brick examples also exist. Wall penetrations are deeply recessed, while horizontal and vertical slots create an egg crate effect. Boston City Hall is the best known example of Brutalist architecture.

Late Modern buildings feature glass curtain wall, and the appearance of a Late Modern building varies greatly from example to example. Philip Johnson, I.M. Pei, and Ceasar Pelli are noted architects of the style; however, by this period in American architecture, design firms became associated with buildings as opposed to individual architects. Skidmore, Owings & Merrill architects is also closely associated with the style.

Post Modernism is another style that falls within the overall Modern category. Buildings reflect the surrounding cityscape or neighborhood, often because architects incorporated classical or vernacular features. Architects grew wary of the non-descript buildings of the mid-twentieth century, and began combing historic precedents with modern building materials. One architectural historian stated that Post Modern buildings are inspired by the clutter of Main Street. Circles and curves are integrated for variety and texture, and many examples exhibit bold, even playful combinations of color. Philip Johnson's AT&T Building in New York City is the most often cited Post Modern building.

Cyclorama Building, Gettysburg, Adams County. Completed as part of the National Park Service's "Mission 66" program, the endangered Cyclorama Building is viewed as a masterpiece of modernist architect Richard Neutra. The building's signature is a massive concrete rotunda that was designed to house the Gettysburg Cyclorama, which has since been relocated to a newer visitors center.

The Ware Center (Pennsylvania Academy of Music Building), Lancaster, Lancaster County. Now part of Millersville University, this modern building was constructed originally for a private music academy. Famed architect Philip Johnson, of Philip Johnson • Alan Ritche Architects, designed the striking building in one of his final design commissions before his death. The North Prince Street building includes a 370-seat recital hall and was completed for a cost of $28 million.

State Museum of Pennsylvania and Archives, Harrisburg, Dauphin County. Lawrie and Green Architects looked to the 1939 World's Fair in New York City for inspiration for these buildings. Their resulting design, which was built in 1963, found its muses in Trylon and Perisphere, two iconic structures from the World's Fair.

Commonwealth Keystone Building, Harrisburg, Dauphin County. One of the newer buildings on the Capitol Complex in Harrisburg, this post-modern building was designed to emulate the older campus buildings but in a contemporary form. Designed by Bohlin Cywinski Jackson, the Indiana limestone and granite building was completed in 2000.

Programmatic & Roadside Architecture

Other Terms: Fantasy; Novelty; Whimsical
Years: 1920 – 1950

Prospect Diner, Columbia, Lancaster County. While Art Moderne buildings are not nearly as widespread as other styles, it seems that most communities have a shiny railcar-inspired diner like Lancaster County's Prospect Diner.

As Americans adopted the automobile as their primary form of transportation, car ownership became more widespread and owners of shops, restaurants, theaters, and hotels built larger-than-life structures to attract attention. Whimsical buildings, massive statues, sleek drive-ins, and flashy neon signs were all used to gain the attention of passing motorists. "Roadside architecture" is not a style – it is a movement, which was prominent from the 1920s through the mid-twentieth century. In many cases, architects designed a building to emulate a particular shape or animal – a duck, shoe, or elephant, for example – and created an interior to match the exterior shape. The original Golden Arch (a massive single arch) and towering Bob's Big Boy statue are well known examples, as are Minnesota's Paul Bunyan/Blue Ox and New Jersey's Elephant House.

By definition, "Programmatic" architecture refers to buildings and structures that are constructed in forms not normally associated with architecture – like an animal or a shoe or even a railcar.

Shiny diners can also fit comfortably into this category. The prefabricated diner has its origins in traveling lunch wagons, which were transplanted by long, narrow diners that were constructed in factories and then transported to locations throughout the northeastern United States, where they were most popular. During the heyday of diners, 1920-1940, most were inspired by railroad dining cars and built in the Art Moderne style.

Because the famed Lincoln Highway cuts through the heart of South Central Pennsylvania, several nationally recognized examples of Roadside Architecture are found here. York County's best example of the movement happens to be one of the most-referenced examples – the Haines Shoe House, which was built to market a chain of shoe stores. Lancaster's Dutch Haven windmill is another iconic Lincoln Highway structure while the single-arch McDonald's sign west of Lancaster is one of the last of its kind in the United States. The castle of Dutch Wonderland east of Lancaster also falls within this architectural category – as do most amusement park buildings. Most communities in South Central Pennsylvania still have prefabricated diners that continue to serve loyal customers after many decades in business.

Dutch Haven, Ronks, Lancaster County. Based upon a traditional Dutch windmill, this eye-catching structure was constructed around an existing building in 1946 by Roy and Alice Weaver.

Haines Shoe House, Hellam Township, York County. The "Shoe Wizard," Mahlon Haines, built the famed Shoe House along the Lincoln Highway in 1948. It is forty-eight feet long and twenty-five feet high. When built, the "shoe" contained seven rooms including a honeymoon suite.

Opposite page:
McDonald's Sign, Lancaster Township, Lancaster County. Only a few of the original single-arch McDonald's signs remain in the country, including this example on the Lincoln Highway west of Lancaster.

Buildings are responsible for 40% of energy consumption in the United States, as well as 39% of carbon dioxide emissions and 13% of water consumption. Historically, buildings were constructed to be "green" – even before the advent of electricity. Thick walls, liberal use of daylight, buildings positioned to take advantage of sun and shade, and recycled materials used for construction are all sustainable design techniques employed today that were used throughout the centuries. The United States General Service Administration studied Federal buildings and found that utility costs for their historic buildings were actually 27% less than the utility costs for their modern buildings. Another study found that buildings constructed prior to 1920 were more energy efficient than buildings constructed between 1920 and 2000.

As populations expanded after World War II, farms gave way to urban sprawl and buildings became less energy efficient. The design and construction industry eventually began to take notice and concluded that there had to be a better way. The U.S. Green Building Council was founded in 1993 to promote sustainable practices in the design, construction, and operation of buildings. The organization pioneered the Leadership in Energy and Environmental Design (LEED) building rating system to provide a framework for sustainable buildings. Points are earned in several categories, including Sustainable Sites, Water Efficiency, Energy and Atmosphere, Materials and Resources, Indoor Environmental Quality, and Innovation in Design. Points are totaled, and buildings with a certain number of points are certified at different levels including Certified, Silver, Gold, and Platinum, which

is the highest level. Buildings do not have to be LEED Certified to be considered green, but it is the most recognized system in the United States for identifying green buildings.

Organic Architecture is "green" by its very nature. The phrase was coined by Frank Lloyd Wright, who believed that buildings should be designed to be in harmony with their surrounding environment. Wright's Fallingwater is the most famous example of Organic Architecture. Today, the term is used to refer to buildings that are integrated with the surrounding environment through use of materials and design features.

There are many examples of Green Buildings in South Central Pennsylvania, including Pennsylvania's "first green building," the Department of Environmental Protection Southcentral Regional Office Building in Harrisburg. New government and educational buildings are frequently designed according to LEED standards, but existing buildings can also be renovated to meet the criteria. The former York County Court House was converted into a government office building and was York City's first LEED Certified building and York County's first historic LEED Certified Building and first LEED Certified renovation. In Harrisburg, a number of state-related buildings are certified at various LEED levels, including the Pennsylvania Housing Finance Agency building on North Front Street. Several educational buildings throughout the area have obtained LEED Certification, including Paradise Elementary School in Lancaster County and Clearview Elementary School in Hanover. The Center for Athletics Recreation and Fitness at Gettysburg College is an example of a regional higher education facility holding LEED Certification.

Paradise Elementary School, Paradise, Lancaster County. Recipient of the 2009 Overall Design Award from the Green Building Association of Central Pennsylvania, Paradise Elementary School obtained LEED Gold Certification from the U.S. Green Building Council and was Lancaster's County's first LEED Certified school.

Kin Residence, Hellam Township, York County. One of South Central Pennsylvania's most unique houses is located on a hill overlooking the Susquehanna River, near Sam Lewis State Park. An example of Organic Architecture, the Kin Residence has walls made from straw bales, bamboo ceilings, and cork flooring. Passive solar heating warms the house in winter while solar panels provide a natural source for heating water. An attractive green roof reinforces the appearance of the house being one with the surrounding environment.

Pennsylvania Department of Environmental Protection Southcentral Regional Office, Harrisburg, Dauphin County. This facility has been touted as Pennsylvania's first green building. Completed in 1998, the model building was developed using a four-point program: (1) utilize high-performance technology to minimize energy consumption, (2) maximize the use of sustainable materials, (3) minimize negative impacts on indoor air quality, and (4) improve health, motivation, and productivity of building users.

Greenway Tech Centre, York, York County. Constructed in 1911, the former Eisenlohr Cigar Factory was renovated and rehabilitated in 2006 as a high-tech loft-style office building. It obtained LEED Silver Certification and the Green Building Association of Central Pennsylvania recognized it with an Overall Award of Excellence.

South Central Pennsylvania is home to many famous bridges. The longest covered bridge in the world, which once spanned the Susquehanna River between Lancaster and York Counties, was destroyed during the Civil War. Today, Lancaster County has twenty-nine covered bridges – more than any other county in the Commonwealth of Pennsylvania.

The Columbia-Wrightsville Bridge, Walnut Street Bridge, and Rockville Bridge are all National Historic Civil Engineering landmarks. In fact, the Rockville Bridge, which spans the Susquehanna River between Cumberland and Dauphin Counties, is recognized as the longest stone masonry arch railroad bridge in the world.

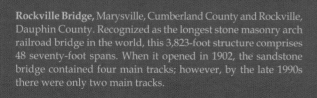

Baumgardeners Bridge, Pequea Creek, Lancaster County. Built in 1860 at a cost of $1,284, this picturesque bridge has a double Burr arch truss design. The bridge was raised by four feet, and lengthened by nine feet, in 1987 to protect it from future flooding.

Rockville Bridge, Marysville, Cumberland County and Rockville, Dauphin County. Recognized as the longest stone masonry arch railroad bridge in the world, this 3,823-foot structure comprises 48 seventy-foot spans. When it opened in 1902, the sandstone bridge contained four main tracks; however, by the late 1990s there were only two main tracks.

Walnut Street Bridge, Harrisburg, Dauphin County. The "People's Bridge," as it is sometimes called, is a truss bridge built by the Phoenix Bridge Company in 1890. Today it connects Riverfront Park with City Island, though for most of its history it also connected to the Cumberland County side of the Susquehanna River. That all changed in 1996 when several sections collapsed as a result of floodwaters carrying ice and debris. The bridge is a National Historic Civil Engineering Landmark and, when whole, was one of the longest pedestrian bridges in the world.

Columbia-Wrightsville Bridge, Columbia, Lancaster County and Wrightsville, York County. Also known as the Veterans Memorial Bridge, this Art Deco-influenced structure is a National Historic Civil Engineering Landmark. The mile-long arched bridge along the Lincoln Highway was completed in 1930 for a cost of $2.5 million. The bridge is over 7,340 feet long and contains twenty-eight 185-foot spans.

Several of Pennsylvania's top agriculture-producing counties are located in South Central Pennsylvania, making sprawling farms and picturesque barns a common part of the landscape. There are many types of barns to be found, but one of the most widespread is known as the Pennsylvania Barn. This category of barn is banked – either set into a hillside or having an earthen ramp built up to the main level of the structure. The lower level contains an overshoot known as a forebay, which overhangs the foundation. Most Pennsylvania Barns have gable roofs.

Another common type of barn is the Sweitzer Barn, which is a barn with an asymmetrical gable roof. This appearance is created by an unsupported overhang on the down slope, creating two sloping roofs of different lengths.

English Barns are typically one story with no basement level or banking. They have a large central door. A subtype of this style is the Basement Barn, which is an English Barn raised over a basement, but still with no banking.

A Three-Gable Barn may be banked or not, but is distinctive in that the main barn has gables on both ends with a large, two-story shed attached at a right angle to the main building. This shed also has a gabled roof, resulting in the aptly-named Three-Gable Barn.

A less-common type of barn is called a Stable Barn or Wisconsin Dairy Barn, named for its purpose: to provide stables for dairy cows. These barns are also sometimes called Gothic Barns because their roof is shaped liked a Gothic arch.

A rare type of barn in South Central Pennsylvania is a Round Barn, which is a term used to describe both polygonal-shaped barns as well as totally circular barns, which are known as Barrel Barns.

The most common forms of barn embellishment in the area are painted decorations known as "hex signs," which are a type of Pennsylvania Dutch folk art. Star shapes are the most frequent decoration, though roses, birds, and other patterns are also widespread. While some people believe that hex signs were once used as talismans to ward against evil – a hex is an evil spell – most historians believe that hex signs are purely for decoration.

Another form of decoration is related to the architecture itself. Barns with brick ends frequently contain patterns in the brickwork, creating openings for light and ventilation. Wheat, diamonds, and rectangles are all types of brick-end patterns.

Centennial Barn, Fort Hunter, Dauphin County. Constructed in 1876 by John Reily, the bank barn on the property of Fort Hunter Mansion and Park exhibits Gothic Revival Details. It was once home to the Fort Hunter Dairy.

Round Barn, Biglerville, Adams County. Round barns are relatively rare, and this barrel barn located west of Gettysburg is truly unique. Designed by Chambersburg architect Morris Rhodes, this barn was built in 1914 for Noah Sheely and his family. The barn's diameter is more than eighty-seven feet and the structure was constructed around a silo standing sixty feet high.

Star Barn, Lower Swatara Township, Dauphin County. The famous Star Barn is a Gothic Revival bank barn constructed in 1872. Named for the decorative stars in the gabled ends and prominent cross gable, the Star Barn was designed by carpenter and mortician Daniel Reichert. The stars are actually wooden louvers that provide light while aiding building ventilation. In 2007, Agrarian Country purchased the National Historic Landmark with plans to relocate the historic barn and outbuildings to serve as an Agricultural Education and Exhibition Center near Grantville, Pennsylvania.

Beasley Barn, Hellam Township, York County. This attractive brick-end barn is located along the Lincoln Highway, west of Hallam. The brickwork patterns contain gaps to let light into the interior spaces while also creating unique decoration for the exterior.

Railroad service arrived in South Central Pennsylvania in the 1830s. The first railroad in Lancaster County was the Philadelphia and Columbia Railroad, which opened in 1834. York County received railroad service in 1838 when the Northern Central Railroad was established, connecting York with Baltimore.

Harrisburg's first train station was built in 1837, and ever since then railroad or train stations have been integral to their local communities. In fact, a number of South Central Pennsylvania train stations are listed on the National Register of Historic Places. During the Civil War, railroads played an important role in transporting Union troops and supplies, and during the Confederate Army invasion in 1863, railroad tracks and bridges were destroyed. They were rebuilt shortly thereafter, allowing soldiers wounded in the Battle of Gettysburg to be transported to hospitals throughout the region. President Abraham Lincoln rode the local rail tracks going to and from Gettysburg to give his famous address. Less than two years later, the Lincoln Funeral Train passed through South Central Pennsylvania.

It was the railroads that allowed the region to grow and prosper, providing means to transport agricultural products and manufactured goods throughout the region and beyond. In fact, the first coal-burning locomotive in the country, the York, which was designed by Phineas Davis, was built and tested in York County.

Harrisburg Central Railroad Station, Harrisburg, Dauphin County. The Harrisburg Central Railroad Station is a National Historic Landmark now known as the Harrisburg Transportation Center. It was built in 1887 by the Pennsylvania Railroad and is Queen Anne in style. Expansions occurred in 1902 and again in 1910. The building is constructed of red brick with Hummelstown brownstone trim.

Gettysburg Railroad Station, Gettysburg, Adams County. The Gettysburg Railroad Station operated from 1852 until 1942, when passenger service ended. The station served the Western Maryland Railway, but is best known for hosting President Abraham Lincoln during his November 1863 visit to deliver the Gettysburg Address. The attractive Italianate building was expanded in 1886 and restored in 2006.

Reading Passenger Station, Lebanon, Lebanon County. Philadelphia's Wilson Brothers and Company, Architects and Engineers, designed this passenger station, which was built in 1900. The eclectic Victorian building is defined by large overhanging roofs and an octagonal tower that stands almost eighty feet above the station.

Hanover Junction Rail Station, Hanover Junction, York County. Located along Route 616 in southern York County, the Hanover Junction Railroad Station was a stopping point for President Abraham Lincoln as he traveled to and from Gettysburg in November 1863. The building was built in 1852 by the National Central Railroad and more than 11,000 wounded were processed through the station in the weeks after the Battle of Gettysburg. Today, it houses a museum and is a stop along Heritage Rail-Trail County Park.

Mills are a common sight in South Central Pennsylvania, due both to the prominence of agriculture in the region as well as the area's legacy of industrial innovation. Many of the early mills were grist mills (or gristmills), which were used to grind grain into flower. They were powered by Mother Nature – some by wind, others by water. The water mills used a water wheel to drive the mechanical processes for flour grinding, lumber production, or even metal shaping. Roller mills were also commonplace throughout the area. These mills housed metal forming equipment in the form of large rollers that pressed the metal.

Many of these mills survive today and have been adapted for other purposes. Some are open to visitors, including the Wallace-Cross Grist Mill in Crossroads, Muddy Creek Forks Roller Mill near Brogue, Clear Springs Mill in Dillsburg, and Mascot Roller Mills in Ronks.

Baumgardner's Mill, Pequea Township, Lancaster County. Built in the early 1800s by Jacob Smith, this water-powered mill was expanded by Abraham Mylin and purchased by Thomas Baumgardner in 1870.

Mascot Roller Mills, Ronks, Lancaster County. The core of this historic building dates to the 1730s, when a small mill was constructed. That mill was expanded in the early-to-mid nineteenth century, and then owned and operated by three generations of the Ressler family beginning in 1865 through 1977. Today the Mascot Roller Mill and Ressler Family Home are a tourist attraction located in the heart of Lancaster's Amish Country.

Wallace-Cross Grist Mill, Crossroads, York County. This grist mill was known to be standing in 1840 and could possibly have been constructed as early as 1826. Alexander Wallace was the original owner, and later Henry Cross, the two men for whom the mill is named. The mill was built of hand-hewn timbers and beams and used water power for its millstone grinding process. Restored by the York County Parks Department, the mill is open to the public.

Anderson Mill, Fawn Township, York County. Also known as Garvine's Mill (or Garvine Mill), the raised stone foundation of this mill dates from the 1780s. After a devastating fire in the 1870s, the upper wood portion was rebuilt above the original foundation. It served as both a cornmeal mill and later a cider mill.

Architectural Terms
Used in this Book

Acanthus
A Mediterranean plant; likeness used for building decoration, most often on column capitals.

Arcade
A covered walkway lined with arches on one or both sides.

Arch
A curved span over an opening, sometimes decorative, sometimes a structural support.

Architrave
The bottom horizontal band of an entablature, found below the frieze.

Ashlar
Rectangular stone blocks, larger than brick.

Balustrade
A grouping of balusters with handrail; that is, a low railing supported by small vertical posts of stone or wood (balusters).

Bargeboard
Decorative woodwork that hangs from the edge of a gabled roof; also known as gableboard.

Basket Handle Arch
A flattened, elliptical-shaped arch.

Battened
A door or shutter with vertical boards held together by battens, or boards fastened across multiple parallel boards to hold them together.

Battered
A sloped or tapered vertical surface narrower at the top.

Battlement
A specialized wall with high and low parapets, originally built for military purposes to provide both protection and an opening to fire arrows.

Bay
Repeated spatial element, particularly windows on a façade; e.g., five evenly spaced windows or four windows and a door both constitute five bays in width.

Bay Window
A window that protrudes from a façade.

Bell Roof
A curved roof flaring out at the ends or eaves; cross-section resembles a bell.

Belfry
A rooftop structure, or portion of a tower or turret, in which bells are hung.

Belt Course
A horizontal band projecting from a façade, usually built of masonry.

Belvedere
A rooftop structure or top level of a tower, accessible by stairs or ladder and from which one can look out. A belvedere has a roof and is open on one or more sides. The term means "beautiful view."

Bond
In brickwork, the pattern of headers and stretchers. The Flemish or Dutch bond consists of headers and stretchers laid alternatively in a course, with the headers in one course centered above the stretchers in the courses above or below. The English bond consists of alternating rows of headers and stretchers, with headers centered on stretchers.

Bracket
A supporting element frequently found below an eave. Brackets can be both functional and decorative.

Cantilever
A surface that projects outward beyond its vertical support.

Capital
The decorated upper portion of a column, pillar, or pilaster.

Casement Window
A single or multi-pane sash, hinged on a vertical side, which usually opens outward.

Castle
A medieval fortified structure.

Cartouche
An ornamental frame or oval, frequently featuring a scroll or figure.

Chateau
Imposing house or castle built in France.

Chicago Window
A large plate glass window with two operable windows on either side.

Chimney Cap
A cornice-like detail on the top edge of a chimney.

Chimney Pot
A decorative, cylindrical pipe atop a chimney.

Chinking
Material used to fill cracks or openings, particularly with log construction. May be of mud, plaster, straw, or sticks.

Clapboard
Exterior wood boards; wedge-shaped in early American construction.

Classical
Related to Greek or Roman architecture.

Colossal
Having more than one story.

Column
A column is a vertical element, usually rounded and most often a structural support. Greek and Roman architecture is categorized by Order, though columns have been used throughout the world by many different cultures in many different times. If the column is physically touching an adjacent wall, or partially built into it, it is said to be "engaged."

Composite
The Composite Order is a hybrid of the Ionic and Corinthian Orders, and its capital (top of column) typically features scrolls and acanthus leaves.

Concave
Curved inward.

Conical Roof
A cone-shaped roof.

Convex
Curved outward.

Corbel
A bracket or block built into a wall to support weight. It can be of any material. A row of corbels is known as a corbel table, which usually occurs below roof eaves and can actually be both decorative and functional.

Corinthian
The Corinthian Order is by far the most ornate, and easily distinguished by the acanthus leaves on the capital (top of column).

Cornerstone
A special building block featuring an inscription, usually a significant date.

Cornice
In general use, the projection at the top of a wall, below the eaves. Specifically, the top horizontal band of an entablature, found above the frieze.

Course
A decorative horizontal band found on an exterior wall. Also known as a stringcourse, this feature is typically stone or brick.

Crenellation
Having battlements.

Cresting
Decorative strap or board along a roof ridge, cornice, or parapet.

Cross Gable
Gable that is perpendicular with the main roof.

Cupola
Cupola means "small cup" and is an architectural feature that resembles a small cup turned upside down. A cupola frequently crowns a roof, dome, or turret. In common usage, cupola is used today to refer to round, square, open, closed, occupied, and unoccupied structures.

Curtain Wall
A lightweight exterior wall.

Dentil
An ornamental tooth-like block, frequently in a series (like a molding) and found under a cornice.

Dichromatic
Having two colors.

Dome
A circular or spherical rooftop structure, though a spherical ceiling is also known as a dome. As an architectural feature, domes come in all sizes and shapes: onion domes, bell domes, saucer domes, etc. Sometimes, "dome" can refer to a cathedral: the Florence Cathedral in Italy is known as the Duomo.

Doric
The Doric Order features a fluted, tapered column with a capital (top of the column) comprising a square abacus and spreading echinus.

Dormer
An architectural feature projecting from a sloping roof and usually containing a vertical-oriented window.

Double-Hung
A window with two sashes that slide vertically.

Eave
The lower portion of a roof projecting over a wall.

Engaged
Attached to a wall or partially embedded.

Entablature
Horizontal bands (architrave, frieze, and cornice) above the structural supports in a building (e.g., columns).

Eyebrow Dormer
A low curved dormer without sides and shaped like an eyebrow.

Façade
The front of a building, or other side with significant architectural merit.

Fachwerk
German half-timbering construction technique.

Fanlight
A semicircular window with ribbed bars, usually over a door or another window.

Fenestration
The arrangement of windows in a building.

Finial
The top of a spire or pinnacle; usually decorative.

Flared
Gradually diminishing slope; spreading outward.

Flat Arch
An arch with a horizontal lower face.

Fleche
French term for spire, though it also refers specifically to a small slender spire.

Flemish Gable
A gable with pediment having two or more curves on each side.

Florentine
Relating to Florence, Italy. Frequently used to reference the Florence Cathedral.

Fluted
Series of vertical grooves, most frequently found in a column.

Foliate
Leaf shaped.

French Doors
Paired doors with glass panes covering most of the door surface.

Fresco
A wall or ceiling painting, typically on plaster.

Fret
A type of Greek ornamentation, also known as a key, with continuous, angular lines.

Frieze
The central horizontal band of an entablature, found below the cornice and above the architrave.

Gable Roof
A sloping roof which resembles an "A." Gable roofs are also sometimes generically referred to as "pitched roofs."

Gambrel Roof
A roof with two slopes on either side, with the lower slope having a steeper pitch than the upper slope.

Gargoyle
A decorative waterspout featuring a lion or grotesque creature.

Glazed Brick
Another term for enameled brick – a brick with a "glassy" or lustrous surface.

Grotesque
Sculptured ornament of fantastical human or animal forms.

Half-Timber
Construction method utilizing timber frames for internal and external walls, with brick and plaster infill between the timbers.

Header
The short surface area of a brick.

Hipped Roof
A roof with all sides sloping upward, typically at a uniform pitch. Frequently found over a rectangular structure. When found over a square structure, it becomes a pyramidal roof.

Hood Mold
Also known as a dripstone, a hood mold projects above a door, window, or arch. It is both decorative and serves a purpose—to divert rain. In modern usage, a hood mold is simply referred to as a lintel.

Ionic
The Ionic Order is easily distinguished by the scrolls (a.k.a., volutes) at the top of the column, known as the capital.

Keep
The inner tower of a castle.

Keystone
A wedge-shaped piece, usually masonry, at the top of an arch, locking all the other pieces in place. Also a decorative piece found above windows.

Lancet Arch
A sharp, pointed arch with two centers.

Lantern
A small structure, either open or with windows, crowning a roof. While it can be decorative, the primary function is to assist with ventilation or provide natural lighting to the space below.

Lintel
Horizontal, weight-bearing member above an opening like a window.

Louver
Horizontal or vertical boards or slats covering a window; exist to allow light and ventilation while keeping out rain.

Mansard Roof
A roof with two slopes; the lower slope is steeper (almost vertical) than the upper slope (almost horizontal).

Masonry
Brick, stone, or concrete, or the work of a mason.

Mission Parapet
A multi-curved parapet.

Modillion
An ornamental bracket or block under the cornice. Similar to a dentil, only larger.

Monochromatic
Having one color.

Monumental
Having a large scale.

Ogee
A pointed arch with reversed curve near the apex.

Onion Dome
A bulbous-shaped dome.

Order
Greek and Roman influenced columns are classified into various orders, including Doric, Ionic, Corinthian, Tuscan, and Composite. Also, the "Colossal" or "Giant" Order is sometimes used to refer to multi-story columns.

Oriel
A bay window projecting from an upper-story and usually supported by a bracket or corbel.

Palladian Window
A three-part window with arched central sash and two smaller side sashes.

Pane
A sheet of glass in a window or door.

Parapet
A low wall along a roofline or balcony. Serves both as protection from falling as well as decorative purposes. A series of alternating low and high parapets is known as a battlement.

Pavilion
A structure projecting from a main façade.

Pediment
A triangular gable found atop a portico, doorway, or window; typically features two gentle slopes.

Pendant
A hanging ornament, usually carved of wood.

Pent Roof
A single sloped false roof located between the first and second floors of a building.

Piano Nobile
The principal level of a building located above the ground or basement level.

Pilaster
A usually decorative, shallow rectangular column built into a wall.

Pinnacle
An ornamental feature of pyramidal or conical shape, frequently topped by a finial.

Pitched Roof
A roof with a slope.

Polychromatic
Having a variety of colors.

Portico
An entrance structure (e.g., a porch) or covered walkway utilizing columns.

Pyramidal Roof
A roof shaped like a pyramid, typically found atop towers.

Quatrefoil
A flower-like pattern with four petals or lobes.

Quoin
Brick or stone corner pieces differing in size, color, shape, and/or material from the adjoining walls.

Recessed
Indented.

Relief
Carved, sculptured, or embossed feature raised above the background plane.

Ribbon
A horizontal band with repeating pattern or windows.

Ridge
The meeting point of the upper edge of sloping roofs.

Rose Window
A large round window with floral-patterned tracery.

Rosette
A decorative element with a floral or foliate design.

Rough Cast
Brick, plaster, or stucco with rough texture.

Rough Cut
Textured, non-smooth surface.

Roundel
A round decorative object or figure.

Rusticated
Masonry feature referring to deep recessed joints between stones, usually creating horizontal bands.

Scroll
Spiral ornamentation.

Shed Roof
Flat roof with inclined plane.

Sidelight
A side window, as in a window on either side of a door.

Sphinx
A figure with the body of a lion and head of a man or hawk.

Spindle
Decorative woodwork with rounded form.

Spire
A decorative element atop a roof, tower or steeple. It is typically narrow, tapered, and/or pointed.

Splayed
Horizontal feature with ends slanted down and inward.

Squat
Short and thick.

Statuary
Free-standing sculpture.

Steeple
A tall structure frequently topped by a spire. In general usage, any tower attached to a church is referred to as a steeple.

Stickwork
Wood boards attached to a building exterior in a horizontal, vertical, or diagonal orientation.

Stretcher
The long, horizontal side of a brick.

Stringcourse
Another term for belt course.

Surround
Structure or decorative element around a door or window.

Swag
A carved ornamental decoration like garland, typically on a building's façade; also known as a festoon.

Terra Cotta
Fired clay. The Italian term means "baked earth." It is somewhat hollow, and thus frequently applied to a brick facing.

Thatched Roof
A roof of straw or weeds.

Through-the-Cornice Dormer
A dormer with lower section on a wall and upper section breaking the cornice line; also called a Wall Dormer.

Tower
A structure of great height when compared with its horizontal dimensions. It may be attached to a building or stand-alone, and is typically taller than the structures around it. A tower may have a roof or be open on the top level.

Tracery
Stone, wood, or iron decorative, curved shapes within a window.

Transom
A horizontal bar over a window or door, or between a window and door.

Trefoil
A flower-like pattern with three petals or lobes.

Triangular Arch
An arch in the shape of a triangle.

Truncated
A roof, usually hipped or gabled, with top cut out to form a flat surface.

Tudor Arch
A four-centered arch.

Turret
A tower-like structure attached to a larger building and beginning above the ground level. Turrets are often ornamental and cylindrical in shape and typically have roofs.

Tuscan
The Tuscan Order is the most basic of all columns, and is plain and unfluted.

Tympanum
The recessed triangular area within a pediment.

Urn
Decorative vase.

Veranda
Covered, open porch or balcony extending along the exterior of a building.

Vernacular
Regional architectural forms and materials.

Water Table
A projecting stringcourse to divert water.

Wheel Window
A large, round window with decorative tracery in spoke-like pattern.

Widow's Walk
Also known as a captain's walk, a widow's walk is a flat roof deck or elevated platform, enclosed by a railing, from which one can look out. Widow's walks are often found on truncated roofs. In legend, the wives of seafaring men would await their return while standing on the roof; alas, sometimes the men didn't return, leaving their widows standing alone.

Wrought Iron
Malleable iron beaten into decorative shapes and patterns.

Style Guides and Architectural Dictionaries

Baker, John Milnes, AIA. *American House Styles – A Concise Guide.* New York, New York: W. W. Norton & Company, 1994.

*Blumenson, John J. G. *Identifying American Architecture, Revised Edition.* New York, New York: W. W. Norton & Company, Inc., 1981.

Burden, Ernest. *Illustrated Dictionary of Architectural Preservation.* New York, New York: McGraw-Hill, 2004.
   Illustrated Dictionary of Architecture – Second Edition. New York, New York: McGraw-Hill, 2002.

Carley, Rachel. *The Visual Dictionary of Domestic Architecture.* New York, New York: Henry Holt and Company, LLC, 1994.

Foster, Gerald. *American Houses: A Field Guide to the Architecture of the House.* New York, New York: Houghton Mifflin Company, 2004.

Harris, Cyril M. *American Architecture: An Illustrated Encyclopedia.* New York, New York: W. W. Norton & Company, 1998.
   Illustrated Dictionary of Historic Architecture. New York, New York: Dover Publications, Inc., 1977.

Howe, Jeffery. *Houses of Worship – An Identification Guide to the History and Styles of American Religious Architecture.* San Diego, California: Thunder Bay Press, 2003.
   The Houses We Live In – An Identification Guide to the History and Style of American Domestic Architecture. San Diego, California: Thunder Bay Press, 2002.

Klein, Mailyn, and David P. Fogle. *Clues to American Architecture.* Montgomery, AL: Starhill Press, 1986.

*McAlester, Virginia, and Lee. *A Field Guide to American Houses.* New York, New York: Alfred Knopf, 1995.

Morgan, Williams. *The Abrams Guide to American House Styles.* New York, New York: Harry N. Abrams, Inc., 2008.

Morrison, Hugh. *Early American Architecture: From the First Colonial Settlements to the National Period.* New York, New York: Oxford University Press, 1952.

*Poppeliers, John C., et al. *What Style Is It? A Guide to American Architecture.* New York, New York: John Wiley & Sons, Inc., 1983.
   What Style Is It? A Guide to American Architecture. Revised Edition. Hoboken, New Jersey: John Wiley & Sons, Inc., 2003.

Rifkind, Carole. *A Field Guide to American Architecture.* New York: Penguin Group, 1980.

Walker, Lester. *American Homes – An Illustrated Encyclopedia of Domestic Architecture.* New York, New York: Black Dog & Leventhal Publishers, 1981.

*Whiffen, Marcus. *American Architecture Since 1780 – A Guide to the Styles.* Revised Edition. Cambridge, Massachusetts: MIT Press, 1999.

denotes use by the National Park Service in the "Architectural Classification Section" of How to Complete the National Register of Historic Places Registration Form.

Regional Architectural References

Butcher, Scott D. *York's Historic Architecture*. Charleston, South Carolina: The History Press, 2008.

City of Lancaster, Pennsylvania. *To Build Strong and Substantial: The Career of Architect C. Emlen Urban*. Lancaster, Pennsylvania: The City of Lancaster, 2009.

Ensminger, Robert F. *The Pennsylvania Barn: Its Origin, Evolution, and Distribution in North America*. Baltimore, Maryland: Johns Hopkins University Press, 1992.

Frew, Ken. *Building Harrisburg: The Architects and Builders 1719-1941*. Harrisburg, Pennsylvania: Historical Society of Dauphin County and Historic Harrisburg Association, 2009.

Historic Preservation Trust of Lancaster County. *Lancaster County Architecture 1700-1850*. Lancaster, Pennsylvania: Historic Preservation Trust of Lancaster County, 1992.

Kauffman, Henry J. *Architecture of the Pennsylvania Dutch Country 1700-1900*. Elverson, Pennsylvania: Olde Springfield Shoppe, 1992.

Kindig, Joe K., III. *Architecture in York County*. York, Pennsylvania: Trimmer Printing Incorporated, 1979.

"Pennsylvania Architectural Field Guide," Bureau for Historic Preservation, Pennsylvania Historic and Museum Commission, http://www.portal.state.pa.us/portal/server.pt/community/architectural_field_guide/2370 (accessed November 28, 2011).

"Pennsylvania Cultural Resources Geographic Information System," Pennsylvania Historic and Museum Commission and Pennsylvania Department of Transportation, https://www.dot7.state.pa.us/ce/Application/ASP/Security/Index.asp (accessed November 28, 2011).

Snyder, John J., Jr. *Lancaster Architecture 1719-1927; A Guide to Publicly Accessible Buildings in Lancaster County*. Lancaster, Pennsylvania: Historic Preservation Trust of Lancaster County, 1979.

Reference Websites

"American Architectural Style," Wikipedia Contributors, http://en.wikipedia.org/wiki/Category:American_architectural_styles (accessed November 28, 2011).

"Architectural Styles Guide," Preservation Directory, http://www.preservationdirectory.com/historicphotogallery/architecturalstylesgalleries.aspx (accessed November 28, 2011).

"Architectural Styles of America Home Page," Dr. Tom Paradis, http://jan.ucc.nau.edu/~twp/architecture/ (accessed November 28, 2011).

"Buffalo as an Architectural Museum," Chuck LuChiusa, http://www.buffaloah.com/a/bamname.html (accessed November 28, 2011).

"House Style Guide and Examples," OldHouse.com, http://www.oldhouses.com/styleguide/ (accessed November 28, 2011).

"How to Complete the National Register of Historic Places Registration Form," National Park Service, http://www.nps.gov/nr/publications/bulletins/nrb16a/ (accessed November 28, 2011).

"Styles in American Architecture," Jeffery Howe, http://www.bc.edu/bc_org/avp/cas/fnart/fa267/amstyles.html (accessed November 28, 2011).

Radnor Township

Haverford Township

Marple

Chester Township

Ridly Township

DELAWARE RIVER

PART OF WEST